Return from the Precipice

BANGLADESH'S FIGHT AGAINST TERRORISM

Return from the Precipice

BANGLADESH'S FIGHT AGAINST TERRORISM

Anand Kumar

INSTITUTE FOR DEFENCE STUDIES & ANALYSES
NEW DELHI

PENTAGON SECURITY INTERNATIONAL
AN IMPRINT OF PENTAGON PRESS

First Published in 2012

ISBN 978-81-8274-697-8

Published by

PENTAGON SECURITY INTERNATIONAL

An Imprint of

PENTAGON PRESS
206, Peacock Lane, Shahpur Jat,
New Delhi-110049
Phones: 011-64706243, 26491568
Telefax: 011-26490600
email: rajan@pentagonpress.in
website: www.pentagonpress.in

In association with Institute for Defence Studies and Analyses, No. 1, Development Enclave, New Delhi-110010. Phone: +91-11-26717983

Printed at Aegean Offset Printers, Greater Noida, U.P.

Contents

Acknowledgements

I am thankful to a large number of people who have been associated with this book from its inception. Space constraints may not allow me to acknowledge everyone individually. Some of them have also expressed a desire to remain anonymous because of the sensitive nature of their professions. However, a volume of this kind is not possible without the help of colleagues and friends. I would like to express my sincere thanks to Dr. Arvind Gupta, Director General, Institute for Defence Studies and Analyses, New Delhi for his encouragement and support to bring out this volume. He was kind enough to go through the first draft of the book. His valuable comments and those of the anonymous referees helped improve the book greatly. I also sincerely thank my colleagues at the South Asia Centre (IDSA) for their supportive role.

Among the people who requested anonymity are intelligence officials in the Northeast and Delhi, members of the armed forces, senior government officers and human rights activists. I have also interviewed researchers, mediapersons, government officials, politicians and academicians in Bangladesh who don't wish to be named. The inputs provided by them have been integrated in many places in the book.

I would also take this opportunity to thank Vivek Kaushik, Assistant Editor at IDSA who put the book through its paces. Special thanks are also due to Dr Kiran Sahni for copy-editing the manuscript text in a professional and timely manner. Mr Rajan Arya and the staff of Pentagon Press also played an important role in publishing this volume on time.

My wife Nisha and children Yashi and Shaurya had to bear with my irregular schedules while the book was being written. This book is dedicated to them.

I hope this volume will contribute to a better understanding of the complex phenomenon of religious extremism and terrorism in Bangladesh and the northeastern region of India. I sincerely hope that the volume encourages South Asian nations to cooperate so that the threat posed by terrorism is not only contained but defeated in the long run.

Anand Kumar

1

Introduction

The image of Bangladesh as a 'moderate Muslim country' was tarnished at the turn of the 20th century. The country known for its Sufi Islam whose war of liberation was based on Bengali nationalism witnessed an outbreak of Islamic radicalism which attacked the very symbols of Bengali culture. The radical elements in Bangladeshi society which had grown in strength were trying to purge the social, cultural and religious life of the people. This was the time when Bangladesh was ruled by the Bangladesh Nationalist Party (BNP) led four-party alliance. This alliance which was in power from 2001-2006, brought disrepute to a country and people known for their moderate ways. The Bangladeshi intelligentsia was discomfited by the path taken by the country's leadership. However of late the Sheikh Hasina led Awami League government has been trying to revive 'the spirit of liberation' and redeem the country's reputation—which is a daunting task.

Religious extremism in Bangladesh did not begin during the BNP led four-party alliance rule. Extremist forces have had a presence in the country since it was East Pakistan. The world only sat up and took notice when the movement assumed a violent character in the early nineties. Terrorism which was an offshoot of this Islamist extremism however constituted just one strand of the terror challenge in Bangladesh, and largely threatened the democratic and political stability of the country. For India it translated into occasional terror attacks in various parts of the country. This created panic among the Indian people who after a point even started questioning the ability of state to deal with them. Although Bangladesh was only a junior player in such attacks where the lead role was played by Pakistan, the attacks emanating from Bangladesh were more widespread. The attacks from the western border were largely limited to Kashmir or at best to Delhi or Mumbai, but groups like the Bangladesh based Harkat-ul-Jihad-al Islami Bangladesh (HuJI-B) attacked urban centres across the country. Several state capitals—Jaipur, Ahmedabad, Bangaluru, Hyderabad, Guwahati and Agartala figured on their terror map. Blasts also took place in Varanasi.

Bangladesh also played a major role in another strand of terrorism which has been raging in Northeast India. Northeast insurgents have been using the territory of Bangladesh since East Pakistan days to launch terror attacks against India. There was a brief lull in their activities when Bangladesh won its liberation from Pakistan. But these forces were back in business after the assassination of Mujib-ur-Rahman on 15 August 1975 in his Dhaka residence.

While delineating the threat posed by Islamic radicalism to Bangladeshi politics and by Indian insurgent groups to Northeast India, the book also focuses on their sources of finance. This book marks an advance over other works on the same topic as it discusses the actions taken by the Sheikh Hasina led Awami League government to counter terrorism. In the past the governments in Bangladesh not only denied the presence of Islamist groups within their territory, they also vehemently protested whenever India raised the issue of Indian insurgent groups using Bangladeshi territory for attacks in Northeast India. In the absence of cooperation on the issue of countering terrorism, the problem largely remained in the realm of speculation.

But now as the Bangladesh government comes out of its shell and cooperates with India and the wider world, many aspects of the problem have become known. The book also makes an assessment as to what extent Bangladeshi cooperation has helped counter-terrorism activities—especially in India's Northeast.

It has also been alleged that Pakistan has used Bangladesh as an operational zone to launch terror attacks in India and fuel insurgency in Northeast India. Both Pakistan and Bangladesh in the past denied this allegation. Now as Pakistan is going through an internal churn because of the threats from Islamist radicals and the deepening economic crisis made worse by the US war on terror in Af-Pak region, several Pakistani institutions like the Inter-Services Intelligence (ISI) and the army which were earlier considered as being unassailable are also facing pressure. The grilling by the judiciary on the issue of the spy agency's mandate and its role in funding politicians both within and outside Pakistan made former ISI chief Asad Durrani confess to the role Pakistan has been playing in fuelling insurgency in India's Northeast. The ISI has now also confessed that they have funded anti-India political parties like the BNP and Jamaat. As a result of these revelations the book is able offer a more convincing account of the nefarious role ISI has played in the past to destabilise India and its Northeast.

The liberation of Bangladesh and the subsequent policy followed by the country towards India has been a matter of debate among a section of Indians. Though Indian security forces and the political leadership along with the people of India take pride in the role they played to help their brethren in erstwhile East Pakistan, a few have been debating whether the liberation of Bangladesh has actually enhanced Indian security or only increased its worries, especially after reports started emanating that Bangladesh was helping Northeast insurgents and that Islamic radicals from Bangladesh were making common cause with similar elements from Pakistan to create internal security problems for India. This book tries to analyse the developments in Bangladeshi politics which took a very different course after the murder of Bangabandhu. This book highlights the attempt of certain forces in Bangladesh to consciously foster a culture that is different from the composite Bengali culture that is common to both countries, so that a different Bangladeshi identity could be created. India never questioned the existence of Bangladesh or its sovereignty, but elements hell bent on creating differences followed certain policies that actually vitiated bilateral relations between the two countries.

Methodology

Both primary as well as secondary sources have been consulted for this book. I have used material dating from 2002 when I first started working on Bangladesh. Media reports from Bangladesh have been given precedence over Indian media reports. Field visits were undertaken in both Bangladesh and Northeast India. During these field visits I interviewed top policy makers, bureaucrats, police officials, intelligence officials, office holders of political parties, journalists, researchers from think tanks and common people. In many cases the identities of some people have not been disclosed as per their request. These interviews were used to corroborate reports appearing in media.

Organisation of the Book

The book starts by discussing revival of Islam-based politics in Bangladesh. This increased emphasis on Islam coupled with certain social processes and external financial and ideological support led to emergence of political Islam in Bangladesh represented by the Jamaat-e-Islami (Jamaat). This so called 'moderate Islamic party' which is the visible face of political Islam in Bangladesh is the subject of discussion in the third chapter. Along with the

Jamaat there are also certain groups in Bangladesh who share the objective of the creation of an Islamic state with Jamaat but are unwilling to wait until society is fully Islamised and have no inhibitions against the use of violence. These Islamist militants and their acts of terror are discussed in the fourth chapter. India's Northeast has been affected by insurgency since India's independence from British rule. For a long time it was suspected that these insurgents were enjoying safe havens in Bangladesh. Various facets of the Northeastern insurgency are discussed in the fifth chapter. The next chapter discusses the financing of Islamist militancy and Northeast insurgency as it is generally believed that this phenomenon cannot survive for long in the absence of regular funding. The seventh chapter discusses, the policy followed by various regimes towards Islamist militants and Indian insurgents. It also discusses the crackdown on terrorists undertaken by the present Sheikh Hasina regime. The book ends by discussing the reasons for the success of the present Sheikh Hasina government in taking actions against terror groups and its likely impact on counter-terrorism in South Asia especially Bangladesh.

2

Revival of Islam-Based Politics

After liberation Bangladesh attempted to chart a new course for itself that was considerably different from its past. The country accepted nationalism, socialism, democracy and secularism as principles of state policy in the new constitution of Bangladesh that was adopted by its Constituent Assembly on 4 November 1972, and promulgated on 16 December, of the same year.[1] The objective behind this was to give a progressive foundation to the emerging nation. But unfortunately Bangabandhu Sheikh Mujib ur Rahman who was supposed to head Bangladesh with these progressive ideals was killed along with most of his family members on 15 August 1975. This also marked the end of the new beginning.

The subsequent political developments in the country resulted in secularism being removed from the constitution and socialism was redefined. In the struggle between Bengali nationalism and Islamic identity the latter now seems to be having an upper hand. These developments have cast a shadow on the future of democracy in Bangladesh, though the country has received a reprieve with the coming to power of the Sheikh Hasina led Awami League government.

The Islamic parties which were despised in Bangladesh for siding with Pakistan during their war of liberation have not only managed to gain acceptance in Bangladesh polity but they are also playing important role in the country's politics. The Jamaat and Islamic Oikya Jote (IOJ) were part of the right wing ruling coalition which was in power from October 2001 to 2006. Unlike the Jamaat the IOJ has openly declared its allegiance to the Taliban and al-Qaeda. The members of IOJ are often members of HuJI too.[2]

Though the use of Islam for political purposes is not new in Bangladesh politics, in recent times it has become a cause for concern because it has given strength to political parties like the Jamaat which terms itself as the "Islamic Democratic Party".[3] They are cadre based political parties and often have close links with many extremist and terrorist groups. The Jamaat follows the ideals of Abu-ala-Maududi, who was not content with a Muslim state but wanted a fundamentalist Islamic state.

The Jamaat is the manifestation of "political Islam" in Bangladesh. But Jamaat is not the only political party which seeks to establish an Islamic state in Bangladesh. There are a variety of other entities which have the same goal. Some want this transition to be made through 'peaceful means' whereas others are impatient and favour a violent transition. The outfits seeking a violent transition have stayed clear of mainstream politics, but others have worked with existing political parties.

The records of Bangladesh government intelligence agencies reveal the existence and activities of about 100 Islamic political parties and organisations since 1976 when the constitutional ban on formation and functioning of organisations based on religion was repealed.[4] The Bangladesh Election Commission statistics show that 30 Islamic political parties and their different factions have contested parliamentary elections since 1979 with manifestos for establishing Islamic rule. Except for the Jamaat, the other Islamic parties together got less than one per cent of the votes in the elections after revival of parliamentary democracy following the fall of autocratic Ershad regime in 1990.[5]

The statistics however could be misleading as Islam based political parties are at present more focused on the Islamisation of the society rather than on winning parliamentary seats. In the process of the identity formation of Bangladeshi Muslims language emerged as a dominant factor for sometime (1947-75) only to be once again overtaken by religious identity. Islam-based politics was revived not only for political purposes by the military rulers but also because there were independent social processes which gave strength to political Islam. The shallow base of secularism is finding it difficult to resist this religious upsurge resulting in many compromises being made by even the hitherto secular parties.

Quest for Identity

The Bangladeshi identity is made up of two distinct parts, the Bengali and the Muslim. The role of these two elements in the formation of Bangladeshi Muslim identity has varied at different times in the history of the country.

Initially, Islam acted as a unifying factor, followed by the Bengali language, after which the two were reconciled.[6] Finally a trend towards radical Islam has appered in the society.

Islam as Unifying Factor

In the first half of the twentieth century, the people of the region were mobilised on the basis of religion. This led to the alienation of the Bengali Muslim population that ultimately resulted in the creation of Pakistan. This period saw the eclipse of old Muslim elite and and the rise of the Hindus because of the Bengal renaissance. During this period the Bengali language and culture were linked to Brahmanic heritage. The Bangla language borrowed a large number of words from Sanskrit. This was difficult for the Bengal Muslims to swallow and they in turn started borrowing from Arabic and Persian language and also started focusing on Islamic scriptural heritage.

The schism between the two major communities became visible in the Bengali Muslim attitude towards the partition of Bengal in 1905 and the Swadeshi movement against the partition. Muslims in general favoured the partition of Bengal and saw the Swadeshi movement as a ploy to serve Hindu communal interests. They feared that as a backward community in united India they would continue to be exploited by Hindu landlords, businessmen and industrialists.

The fear of Hindu dominance made the East Bengal Muslims take shelter under the banner of Islam and support the Muslim League, which championed the cause of Islam and Muslims in India. This support was crucial to bring about the creation of Pakistan in 1947 on the basis of the two- nation theory. Pakistan was seen as a homeland for Muslims where they would get the opportunity to progress.

However, the sustained campaign for Pakistan under Jinnah also sharpened the communal identity among a section of the population despite the prevailing Sufi tradition of Islam in Bangladesh. The political developments in post-liberation Bangladesh unfortunately have failed to remove this distrust between the communities. This also prepared ground for the emergence of militant Islam in the country.

Language as Unifying Force

From 1947 to 1975 the Bengali language was the unifying factor in East Pakistan (Bangladesh since 1971). The ruling elites in Pakistan distrusted Bengalis and promoted their cultural assimilation by imposing Urdu on the region. Bengalis were however unwilling to give up their mother tongue which also signified their Bengaliness. This struggle gave rise to Bengali nationalism in East Pakistan.

Bengalis were not given much say in the decision making process in the power structure of Pakistan. The state followed a policy of centralised administration and monopolised political power. This also resulted into skewed economic development and created disparity between the two parts of Pakistan.

The formation and development of Awami League as a political party in 1949 was the result of the growing discontent among the Bengali population. The severe defeat of Muslim League in the general elections of 1954 encouraged the Awami League to put greater emphasis on political and economic issues. They started talking of creating an exploitation free society. The Awami League now wanted a fundamental change in the power structure of Pakistan.

In the 1970 general elections, the Awami League won a landslide victory, securing 160 of the 162 seats in East Pakistan. In this election Islam-based political parties could not get any seat but they still polled about 17 per cent of the votes. Despite this massive victory Sheikh Mujib-ur-Rahman was prevented from becoming the prime minister of Pakistan.

What was worse, in 1970 a severe cyclone struck in Bhola district in which nearly half a million people died. But the ruling elite of West Pakistan did not care for them. In fact, when the unrest in East Pakistan was brought to the notice of Zulfikar Ali Bhutto, he remarked that Pakistani forces would go there and kill 20,000 people, after which things would be under control.[7] It has also been pointed out that while there was shortage of grain in East Pakistan, the ruling elite of West Pakistan allowed export of grain. This was highly callous attitude.

The Pakistani state violated the principle of equality of opportunity and the people felt exploited in the name of Islam. By 1971, language had replaced religion as the society's organising principle and became a powerful instrument for nation-building in Bangladesh.

Mujib had championed the cause of a secular state as opposed to an Islamic state. Secularism also became important as a reaction against the orthodox Muslims who had sided with Pakistani forces during the liberation struggle. This change in nature of politics however made India important and underlined its important role in the Liberation War of Bangladesh. Mujib saw Muslims in Bengal linked with Bengali and not West Asian culture.

But a secular Bangladesh was a problematic concept which threatened

Bengali Muslims' quest for a unique identity.[8] The community was now faced with dilemma that: if the unifying factor was Bengali culture and language then what was the need to exist separately from West Bengal and India.

The concept of secularism in Bangladesh also faced problems because its root did not run deep. Though lot of emphasis was placed on secularism during the Bangladesh liberation movement, its main support base was limited only to a small section of the country's liberal elite composed of the academics, Bengali nationalists, political activists, social workers, reformists, writers, singers, artists, lawyers, sections of professionals, journalists, politicians, and feminists.[9] Most of them come from the upper strata of society. They had participated in the nationalist movements before 1947 and in the subsequent liberation war of 1971. The leadership of this liberal elite came from the intellectuals in Dhaka University. The Bengali economists working there highlighted the economic disparities between the two wings of Pakistan. For this they had to face the brutality of Pakistani army in March 1971.

The liberals were secular nationalists who advocated the promotion of Bengali language and culture; the independence and sovereignty of Bangladesh; secularism; individual freedom, and liberal democratic institutions. They were opposed to religious orthodoxy and were committed to modernisation, development, and the progress of women.[10]

While the base of liberals in Bangladesh was a narrow one, the Islamic parties had significant support in the country. This was evident from the fact that even at the height of the anti-Pakistan upsurge during the 1970 general elections these parties managed to get 17 per cent of the total votes in East Pakistan, though they could not win even a single seat in the National Assembly. The failure of the Mujib government to deal sternly with war criminals—the Jamaat, Rajakars, Al Badr Al Shams et al—who had collaborated with the Pakistani army and his decision to provide them amnesty ensured that they could gather strength at a later date. The repatriation of Bengali military officers from West Pakistan and their integration in influential positions within the Bangladesh military structure enormously boosted the morale and spirit of the pro-Pakistan, anti-liberation forces in the country.

The shallow base of secularism in Bangladesh could not have curbed the desire of the Bengali Muslim community for a separate identity. The rift created by the communal movements of pre-partition days was weakened but did not disappear. Religion once again regained its importance in the country's politics as the political parties and politicians of all hues in

Bangladesh tried to consolidate their power base. This also did not allow secularism to develop as a political culture in Bangladesh.

Attempt to Redefine Bangladeshi National Identity

The exploitation of Bengalis by the West Pakistan elite made them look askance at religion as the basis of state formation, but emphasis on Bengali culture and language brought them closer to Hindus, India and West Bengal questioning the raison d'être of their separate existence. This also once again created a problem of identity for Bengali Muslims.

As a result of this dilemma Bangladeshis felt that their relations with India especially West Bengal must be carefully regulated. The help of India in the liberation war was seen as having been motivated. India was also seen as seeking to dominate the internal and external policies of Bangladesh and could also have territorial designs. It could threaten the riverine economy of Bangladesh by cutting off the headwaters of the shared rivers. Separation from West Bengal was also needed to protect the distinct culture of Bangladesh. It was feared that a culturally more developed West Bengal could have easily overwhelmed the cultural development of Bangladesh.

Despite the fact of Mujib being in power the great expectations of free and open cultural relations between Bangladesh and India were belied within a year of the birth of Bangladesh. After Mujib's assassination in 1975 this cultural policy noticeably shifted away from secularism and even further from the unity of Bengali culture, towards a policy of discovering and constructing a Bengali Muslim cultural heritage.

After 1975 there was an attempt to redefine the Bangladesh national identity. Mujib believed that there was a Bengali cultural heritage that was common to both the Hindus and Muslim of West Bengal and Bangladesh. But after him the common Bengali language was used to construct different cultural identities. A section of Bengali Muslims believe that they are speaking Bengali just because they are living in Bengal. Until the first quarter of twentieth century the Ulema were the leaders of Bengali Muslims, and for them Islam was everything. Even the Pan-Islamic movements of the sub-continent that reached the masses through the medium of Bengali, promoted Islamic identity and loyalty to the Umma, and not kinship for the Sanskritising Bengali culture.

After the assassination of Mujib there was a shift in the cultural policy of Bangladesh to create a Bengali Muslim identity by reconciling the Bengali and Muslim aspects of the large majority of the population. There was an attempt to cleanse the Bengali language of terms laden with overtly Hindu religious or Sanskritic imagery. With regard to the Bengali cultural heritage there was a greater emphasis on highlighting and promoting the contribution made by Bengali Muslims. There was also renewed emphasis in the public media on Islamic symbolism which had declined during Mujib period. When General Zia-ur-Rahman took over power in 1975, he mandated that all citizens of the country be known as Bangladeshis and not Bengalees. This was done ostensibly to draw a distinction between Bangladesh citizens and the Bengali speaking nationals of India.[11]

A section in Bangladesh started criticising the Awami League government and its leader, Sheikh Mujib-ur-Rahman, for professing secularism which they perceived as an Indian ploy to increase Hindu influence. This anxiety of Bangladeshi Muslims to emphasise their separate identity marked the beginning of opposition politics in Bangladesh. This politics was often characterised by anti-Indian feeling. The Islamic consciousness among the majority of Bengali Muslims was enhanced. Muslim cultural embers from the past were reignited all over the country to keep the masses religiously stirred. There was also a rising trend in the upper middle class of assimilating Islamic values.

Towards Radical Islam

The Bangladeshi nationalism propagated by Zia and the BNP brought the focus back on Islam. After 1975 Bangladeshi Islam was exposed to Wahabi and Salafi Islam through migrants who were working in West Asia. Similar Islam was also propagated by various Islamic NGOs who were getting their funding from West Asia and North Africa. This strand of Islam despises the syncretic culture of Sufi Islam. The radicals now wanted a complete break from the Bengali culture. This desire made them attack the symbols of Bengali culture. This trend was seen during the rule of four-party alliance. What is worse, they are even threatening democracy and want Bangladesh to be an Islamic state.

Islamisation of Polity Under Zia and Ershad

After the liberation of Bangladesh it was felt that separation of religion from politics would end the exploitation of religion by vested interests. The 1972 constitution not only declared secularism as a fundamental principle of state policy it also prescribed certain measures for its implementation. The constitution talked of the abolition of all forms of communalism, no political recognition of any religion by the state, no exploitation of religion for political ends, and no discrimination on religious grounds.

However, the brief journey of Bangladesh on the road to secularism ended with the assassination of Sheikh Mujibur Rahman on 15 August 1975. This was further ensured with the killing of four other senior national leaders in the Dhaka Central Jail three months later. The change became visible even during the regime of Mushtaque who was president of Bangladesh for 22 months in 1975. Some of the measures he initiated included the scrapping of Mujib's one- party system, a move away from secularism, India and the USSR, the re-building of links with Pakistan, and a furthering of relationships with the Islamic world.[12]

When General Zia-ur-Rahman became the Chief Martial Law Administrator, he successfully used the Islamist parties to strengthen himself. This also prompted him to modify the secular character of the Bangladeshi constitution. He replaced secularism by the phrase "absolute trust and faith in Almighty Allah" and redefined "socialism," as "economic and social justice."[13] Zia inserted Bismillah-ir-Rahman-ir-Rahim (In the Name of Allah, the Beneficent, the Merciful) in the preamble of the constitution and deleted Article 12, which contained the mechanisms for implementation of the principle of secularism. A new clause was added to Article 25, declared the intentions of the state for "stabilising, preserving and strengthening fraternal ties with the Muslim states on the basis of Islamic solidarity."

The banned communal and fundamentalist political parties were legitimised and relationship with Pakistan, Saudi Arabia and the rest of the Muslim world was strengthened. The Bangladeshi nationalism was evolved and popularised emphasising its Islamic content with the objective to create distance from India. The Bangladesh Nationalist Party (BNP) formed by Zia comprised leading cadres of the Muslim League and other pro-Islam parties as a counter to the Awami League and other left-of-centre secular political groups. He also brought some of the leaders of Islam-based political parties into the political limelight. A large component of Zia's Bangladesh Nationalist Party (BNP) was recruited from the former Muslim League and Shah Azizur Rahman, one of the prominent Muslim League leaders, became prime minister. Maulana Mannan, one of the leaders of Bangladesh Jamiatul Muderressin (BJM) was appointed minister of education. The rightist political forces were further appeased with the termination of the Collaborators Act, which permitted prosecution for the crime of collaboration with the Pakistan army during the liberation war. Zia also wooed the newly affluent West Asians.

Zia also took several symbolic measures like hanging posters with quotations from the Quran, in government offices, displaying Quranic verses and Prophet's advice in public places, flying Eid-Mubarak festoons beside the national flags on Eid festivals, messages issued by the head of state or government on religious occasions such as I'd-i-Miladunnabi, Shab-i-Barat, and Muharram, and offerings of munajat (prayer) on special occasions. State media was used to propagate Islam and the principles of Sharia. The government also made itself responsible for the azan (call to prayer) five times a day.

The Zia government created a new Division of Religious Affairs, under a full-fledged minister. The small Islamic Academy was converted into an Islamic Foundation with extensive research facilities. The government also set up an Islamic University with an Islamic Research Centre attached to it. Zia also started prefacing his public speeches with Bismillah-ir-Rahman-ir-Rahim. Bangladesh now became an important member of the Organisation of Islamic Conference (OIC) and the three-member Al-Quds Committee and Islamic Solidarity Front.

The trend of Islamisation was continued during the regime of General Ershad who wanted the principles of Islam to be incorporated in the constitution of Bangladesh. He established a Zakat Fund and the education policy proposed by him included the introduction of Arabic and Islamiat in the schools. He asserted that the cultural life of the Bangladeshis would be firmly based on Islamic principles. He made frequent visits to various shrines and mosques and gave them liberal grants. He used to address the Juma (Friday) congregations and finally got the eighth amendment to the constitution declaring Islam as the state religion of Bangladesh passed by the Jatiya Sangsad (national assembly) on 7 June 1988. The close ties between Bangladesh and the Muslim countries of West Asia promoted by Zia-ur-Rahman greatly strengthened the Islamists and the process of the Islamisation of the Bangladeshi polity. Liberal flows of petrodollars from West Asia resulted in the mushrooming of mosques and madrassas in every nook and corner of the country.

Internal Social Processes and Islamic Upsurge

The Islamic upsurge taking place since mid 1970s has also been due to certain social processes taking place within the Bangladeshi society. They supplemented what military rulers—Generals Zia-ur-Rahman and Ershad—tried to do through state power.

Growing Activities of Religious Institutions and Organisations

Bangladesh is a predominantly Muslim country where a large number of religious institutions and organisations have been engaged in the preaching of the Quran and the Sunnah. They also train a large number of people to carry out this work. These Islamic NGOs have played an important role in the rising tide of Islam. These organisations are of three types. In the first category are the madrassas, mosques and the Tablig Jamaat. In the second category are the centres established around the mazars (tombs) of famous Sufis and saints that are used widely for prayer and meditation, and the third consists of the numerous socio-religious and cultural organisations whose primary function is social welfare but who also work for promotion of Islam.

The traditional religious education in Bangladesh is provided by the madrassas. They have grown in number after the liberation of the country and have better infrastructure. They train the Imams of mosques and teachers of Arabic and Islamiat in schools and colleges. In Bangladesh there are two types of madrassas—Aliya and Qaumi. Qaumi madrassas have proliferated over the last few years leading to rise in extremism.[14] Unlike Aliya madrassas these madrassas are outside government control and provide only religious education. Their total number has crossed the 10,000 mark. These madrassas are a major factor in the rise of Islamic extremism in Bangladesh. They spend a large share of their funds for arms training as part of preparations for 'jihad'. No doubt, poverty is a major reason why people send their children to madrassas, but there are other factors also which prompt them to do so. There is a strong religious belief among the Muslims that if they send their children to madrassas they will go to heaven. A large number of people also believe that Islamic and Quranic education is good for their children.[15]

The madrassas have been a major source of recruits to Islamist and extremist groups. They provided nearly 5000 people for waging jihad against the Soviet occupation army in Afghanistan. These Bangladeshi jihadis also received training in the process. After the withdrawal of Soviets from Afghanistan they returned to their country and are working towards creating an Islamic order in the country.[16]

The thousands of mosques in Bangladesh are active centres of socio-religious activity. The facilities existing in these mosques have vastly improved in last couple of decades as funds have poured in from rich West Asian and North African countries. The activities of these mosques are coordinated by organisations like the Bangladesh Masjid Mission, Masjid Samaj, and Baitush Sharaf.

The Tablig Jamaat religious movement has also played an important role in the Islamic upsurge. The Tablig Jamaat which was established in the early 1940s holds a religious gathering near Dhaka every year in which nearly one million people participate. Generally top leaders of Bangladesh also take part in this gathering. Though it does not have a well-organised institutional framework, but it holds meetings, seminars, and symposiums at the Kakrail Mosque situated almost in the heart of Dhaka, drawing huge crowds.

The promotion of Islam is also being done by a number of socio-religious and cultural organisations. Prominent among these are the Islamic Foundation, Bangladesh Masjid Mission, Islam Prachar Samity, Quranic School Society, Bangladesh Islamic Centre, Bangladesh Jamiatul Muderressin, World Islam Mission (Quran and Sunnah), Ittehadul Ummah, and the Council for Islamic Socio-Cultural Organisations.

The religious sensibilities of the people were also taken into account by the Awami League after liberation. Though the party banned all religion based parties, it allowed formation of Sirat committees for the observance of Eid-e-Milad-un-Nabi throughout the country and retained the study of Arabic and Islamiat in the school curriculum. It also strengthened the functioning of the Islamic Academy. The practice of commencing radio and television programmes and state functions with recitations from the Quran and the holding of receptions on Eid days continued as before.

The ban on the Islam-based political parties in the immediate aftermath of liberation prompted them to extend and intensify their religious activities. They started forming large scale Sirat committees for the celebration of Eid-e-Milad-un-Nabi and the holding of large gatherings on such occasions as the Shab-e-Barat and Muharram. These parties used this base to their advantage when President Zia came to power. The economic depression in the country and attendant unemployment prompted people to throng to the dargahs and khankas of Sufis and Pirs in large numbers.

The economy of Bangladesh was in a terrible condition by the middle of 1974 forcing the government to look for aid. This aid came from the Middle East and North African countries whose economies were thriving due to energy exports. Many of them started financing missionary programmes in various Muslim countries. This led to the proliferation of Islam-based institutions and organisations. The number of mosques and madrassas also increased phenomenally. This inflow of funds also rejuvenated some of the Islam-based political parties in Bangladesh. The growth of Salafi and Wahabi extremist ideology was also due to this.[17]

Islam-Based Political Parties

Islam based political parties existed even in East Pakistan and had significant following. Towards the end of the liberation war the Pakistani military government tried to enlist the support of some Bengalis and Biharis to resist the Bangladeshi freedom fighters. The Biharis had migrated to East Pakistan during the partition. The Bengalis were mostly followers of the Jamaat and Muslim League. They joined paramilitary groups such as the Al-Badars, or Razakars and helped the Pakistan military in its attacks on the Mukti Bahinis (freedom fighters). The Jamaat leaders and their followers were also active in the Shanti (peace) Committees which were created by the Pakistani military with the same objective.

These right-wing militias were involved in the killings of freedom fighters and a number of intellectuals in December 1971. They also committed various atrocities on the Bangladeshi population resulting in their ban in the country.

Proliferation of Islamic Parties During Military Rule

When government control was relaxed after the first martial law period in 1975 and limited opportunities were provided to political parties under the Political Parties Regulations Act of 1976, there were only a few Islamic-based political parties. The government recognised only three of them—the Muslim League, the Council Muslim League, and the Islamic Democratic League. The number of such parties has increased since then, the more prominent among them being the Muslim League, Islamic Democratic League, Jamaat-i-Islam, Nizam-i-Islam Party, Jamiat-e-Ulema-e-Islam, Islamic Republican Party, Bangladesh Justice Party, and the Bangladesh Khilafat Andolon. Most of these parties are led by fundamentalists.

These Islamic parties are also politically motivated and the Jamaat—is the most important among these groups. The Jamaat also has several front organisations and cultural associations. The Islamic Chhatra Shibir is the student wing of Jamaat. There are also several other fringe groups that support and cooperate but are not identical with the Jamaat on broader Islamic movements. These are Islamic Oikya Jote, the Islamic Constitution Movement, Khilafat Majlish, National Musalli Committee, Ahl-e-Hadith, Ulema Committee, Islamic Chatra Sena, Jamiatul Modarassin (Madrassa Teachers' Association), Nezami-i-Islam, and the Muslim League.

Core Ideology

The Islamist radicals in Bangladesh like Islamists elsewhere want to go back to Quran and the Sunna which they consider as original source of teachings. They too believe the Muslims have gone downhill whenever they have deviated from the fundamental teachings of the Quran and the Sunna. This decline could only be arrested by reviving the Islamic code of conduct in public and private lives. To achieve this objective they seek to make Bangladesh an Islamic state.

The Islamist outfits advocate the principles of Islamic justice and the Sharia. These parties demand that existing laws should be modified to conform with the injunctions of the Quran and the Sunnah and that no law repugnant to the injunctions of Islam should be passed in Bangladesh. These parties also stand for closer bonds of unity among the Muslim states.

They want the government to curtail the progressive activities of NGOs which in their view are anti-Islamic. They want the Ahmadias to be declared as non-Muslims. They also want the government to ban newspapers and publications which they consider as anti-Islamic. A section of the religious right owes allegiance to Pakistan and bemoans its break-up.

The Islamic parties get their recruits from mosques and madrassas. But they also have their followers among businessmen, professionals, civil servants, and the military. Of late their following has increased tremendously in the various universities of Bangladesh. They have strong student as well as teachers' unions.

Islam-Based Political Parties No Longer Defensive

The Islam based political parties have managed to revive after the lifting of the ban in 1976. In the immediate aftermath of liberation war they were hated and most of their leaders were either exiled or they went underground. But their fortunes have dramatically changed since 1975 and the Islamic ideologues and their activists are no longer on the defensive. The Jamaat now has a significant political presence in Bangladesh and is presently in alliance with the BNP. It even claims that the Awami League too has sought its support on various occasions. They have emerged as an important player on the political scene of Bangladesh. During elections the Islam based political parties and centre rights parties especially the BNP unite against the secular and liberal parties. An integral part of Bangladeshi nationalism was over emphasis on Islam. Though initially it was used to legitimize Zia's rule, it gave strength to Islamist ideology. At present Bangladeshi nationalism and Islamist ideology seem to be living together.

Notes

1. "The Constitution of Republic of Bangladesh," Government of Bangladesh, Ministry of Law, Dhaka, 1972, p. 5.
2. Alex Perry, "Deadly Cargo," *Time*, 14 October 2002, at http://www.time.com/time/magazine/article/0,9171,364423,00.html

3. A top Jamaat leader defined his party in these terms in an interview with the author.
4. Shakhawat Liton, "Islamic parties boom after 1976 ban lifting: Record shows about 100 organisations exist," 29 August 2006 at http://www.thedailystar.net/2006/08/29/d6082901022.htm
5. Ibid.
6. Aspects of Cultural Policy in Bangladesh, Jnanbrata Bhattacharyya, *Economic and Political Weekly*, Vol. 18, No. 13 (Mar. 26, 1983), pp. 499-502.
7. Pakistan's leaders should heed the lesson of Bangladesh, at http://www.guardian.co.uk/commentisfree/2010/aug/15/pakistan-flood-warning
8. Aspects of Cultural Policy in Bangladesh, Jnanbrata Bhattacharyya, *Economic and Political Weekly*, Vol. 18, No. 13 (Mar. 26, 1983), pp. 499-502.
9. M. Rashiduzzaman, "The Liberals and the Religious Right in Bangladesh," *Asian Survey*, Vol. 34, No. 11 (Nov., 1994), p. 976.
10. M. Rashiduzzaman, "The Liberals and the Religious Right in Bangladesh," *Asian Survey*, Vol. 34, No. 11 (Nov., 1994), pp. 976-79.
11. M. Rashiduzzaman, "Political Unrest and Democracy in Bangladesh," *Asian Survey*, Vol. 37, No. 3 (March, 1997), pp. 267-68.
12. Bangladesh after Zia: A Retrospect and ProspectAuthor(s): Marcus Franda Reviewed work(s): Source: *Economic and Political Weekly*, Vol. 16, No. 34 (Aug. 22, 1981), p. 1392
13. Ahmed Shafiqul Huque and Muhammad A. Hakim, Elections in Bangladesh: Tools of Legitimacy, *Asian Affairs*, Vol. 19, No. 4 (Winter, 1993), p. 251.
14. Bertil Lintner, "Bangladesh Extremist Islamist Consolidation," *Faultlines*, Vol. 14, New Delhi, July 2003.
15. Based on interview conducted during the field visit.
16. Bibhuti Bhusan Nandy, "Whither Heading Bangladesh? The tale of an emerging Islamic monolith," *Dialogue*, October-December, 2008, Vol. 10, No. 2.
17. "Islam in Bangladesh: Revivalism or Power Politics?," Emajuddin Ahamed and D.R.J.A. Nazneen, *Asian Survey*, Vol. 30, No. 8 (Aug., 1990), pp. 795-808.

3

Jamaat-e-Islami: Fountainhead of Extremism

The Jamaat-e-Islami was founded in British India in 1941 by Abu-ala-Maududi who remained its Amir (chief) till 1972. He is considered to be the chief ideologue of the party and all Jamaat members are expected to study his writings. Maududi was of the view that the best way of transforming any society is to train a core group of highly disciplined dedicated and well-informed members to assume leadership in social and political matters. Over time, he hoped that the group would be able to Islamise the entire society after which the Jamaat would push for an Islamic state. Thus originally the Jamaat was an organisation for educated, elite men. However, later it opened up the membership to men and women of other classes as part of deliberate strategy.

Interestingly, Maududi was not in favour of the creation of Pakistan. But he moved there because he thought that the country's secular leadership was 'ignorant of the Islamic Sharia, and would not allow Islam to have a public role. He hoped that, over time, he would be able to transform Pakistan into an Islamic state. Maududi projected himself as a pro democracy activist when the army seized national political power in Pakistan. He opposed army rule because he thought the top army generals were too westernised.

Jamaat started its work, in what is now Bangladesh in the 1950s. It laid emphasis on Islam and remained committed to the unity of Pakistan. As a result Jamaat chose to ignore the grievances of people of East Pakistan and was also unsympathetic towards the ethnic and linguistic sentiments of the region. The blind commitment to the unity of Pakistan prompted Jamaat to support the central government under General Yahya Khan in 1971 who used brute force to suppress the Bengali nationalist movement.

Jamaat became notorious in Bangladesh for collaborating with the Pakistani army during the liberation war. It also indulged in mass rapes and killings for which its leaders are now facing trial. Jamaat was outlawed in independent Bangladesh for its role during the liberation war and also because the country was established as a secular socialist republic. But its workers reorganised themselves in May 1972 and "quietly worked for Islam till 1979."[1]

Jamaat describes itself as a "moderate Islamic political party." The party emerged in its traditional form in May 1979 after the withdrawal of the Political Parties Regulation.[2] It has participated in almost all the national and local elections. Jamaat prefers to adopt 'constitutional means' to attaian its objectives.[3] The government of Bangladesh in 1973, by a notification disqualified Professor Ghulam Azam, a former Amir of Jamaat, from being a citizen of Bangladesh. But now this ban has been repealed.

The collaboration of the Jamaat with Pakistan army and the involvement of its leaders in war crimes created an image problem for the party. In the immediate aftermath of liberation it was a challenge for the party to convince the people that the Jamaat was not opposed to the independence and sovereignty of Bangladesh.

The Jamaat has now undertaken an extensive propaganda campaign to refurbish its image. The Jamaat now says that it was not the only political party that supported the cause of united Pakistan. There were other parties namely, the Muslim League, Nezam-e-Islam Party, Jamiyat Ulema Islam, the pro China Communist Party all of whom supported the cause of united Pakistan. It also claims that a large number of prominent personalities had taken similar stand.[4]

In subsequent years, the Jamaat slowly become a full participant in the political process, rehabilitated by generals Zia-ur-Rahman and Hussain Muhammad Ershad. The primary motivation however of the authoritarian rulers in Bangladesh was to bolster their own political legitimacy through their much-publicised support for Islam.

Organisation of Jammat

Jamaat-e-Islami is the best organised outfit among all the Islam-based political parties in Bangladesh. Its structure is similar to revolutionary cadre-based parties where members move up through concentric circles of cells. Its cadres are disciplined. The party has a highly selective membership process. A prospective party member begins as an associate and receives lessons in party ideology before being conferred full membership. Unlike other parties, Jamaat has developed a stable party fund and contributions come from members and sympathisers. The influence of Jamaat now is quite widespread. Its sympathisers are of all ages, some of whom are madrassa educated but others have also received a modern education.

Ideology

The aim and objective of the Jama'at is:

> nothing but to achieve the pleasure of Allah and the success in the life hereafter through allround struggle **to establish Islamic order** revealed by Allah and exemplified by his last Prophet, so that mankind may enjoy peace, prosperity, security and progress.[5]

The Jamaat claims to be a "religious, social, political and cultural party which embraces Islam in its entirety without any reservation."[6] The party thinks that "constitutionally Bangladesh is neither Islamic nor socialist. It is secular in the sense that the Quran and Sunnah have not been declared as the principal sources of law, though Islam has been declared as the 'state religion'."[7]

The Jamaat's Idea of an Islamic State

The Jamaat like all other Islamist organisations believes in the idea of Islamic state. But it has tried to camouflage this by the use of modern terminology. It says that the Islamic state is a "welfare state, a multi-religious, multi-cultural and democratic state run by the people's representatives."[8] But its true nature comes immediately to the fore when it says that:

> its principles (of Islamic state) are derived from the Holy Quran and Sunnah of Prophet Muhammad (SM) but its administration is carried out by the representatives of the people. The form of the Islamic government is a divine democratic government because the Muslims have been given limited popular sovereignty under the suvereinty of God. The executive power under this system of government is constituted by the general will of the Muslims who have also the right to depose it. The sources of law of the Islamic state are as follows; (1) The Holy Quran (2) The Sunnah (the practice and sayings of the prophet) (3) The third source of law is the Ijma of the companions of the Prophet. (4) Ijtihad. The constitution of the state must follow the rules of the Holy Quran and Sunnah. It is a divinely ordained system

> of laws. The Quranic law is supreme. Sunnah occupied second position as the source of law.[9]

Clearly the Islamic state as envisaged by the Jamaat is very different from a modern democratic state.

Jamaat's Strategy to Increase Influence

The Jamaat is moving in a systematic way to increase its influence in Bangladeshi society so that its objective of Islamic state can be achieved. It has taken a number of steps for this purpose.

Indoctrination through Party and other Front Organisations

Though the Jamaat exists as a separate organisation it also operates through a number of front organisations such as Islami Chhatra Shibir (ICS) and Islami Yubo Shibir and other religious-cultural organisations such as the Bangladesh Masjid Mission and the Bangladesh Islamic Centre. The party is not keen to immediately capture state power because it believes that it would not last long unless it is effectively backed by an Islamic society. This is why it is trying to inculcate a Islamic consciousness among the people through seminars, symposiums, discussion groups, work camps, and social activities. It emphasises character building and disciplined living. The Jamaat and its front organistions have international contacts with similar organistions, particularly with those in Saudi Arabia, Pakistan, and Malaysia. The influence of Jamaat and its affiliate organisations has been continuously increasing in Bangladesh. The Islami Chhatra Shibir now has a major presence in several universities and is one of the strongest student fronts.

Madrassa Education

The Jamaat is using madrassas to increase its influence in Bangladeshi society. It is also trying to change the notion that madrassas are for the poor as they provide free boarding and lodging. To attract the elite it has set up English medium madrassas.[10] They also have madrassas exclusively for women. These madrassas are being used to indoctrinate women with Islamist ideology. They will ultimately prove to be an important tool for the Jamaat to spread its ideology.

Though madrassas are a major factor in the rise of extremism this phenomenon is not restricted only to them. Now several think tanks in Bangladesh believe that Islamic militant organisations are recruiting a large number of people from the mainstream education syatem.[11] Shibir cadres are coming from universities. A large number of them are science graduates from Dhaka University. The Jamaat as part of the previous ruling coalition has infilterated into universities. It has recruited its party cadres as professors and allocated seats to the students in hostels who follow its ideology.[12]

Jamaat Targeting Women

Jamaat-e-Islami in Bangladesh is now planning to expand its base among women. Though Maududi had stated that women's divinely ordained place was in the home, the Jamaat in Bangladesh finds itself in circumstances that are substantially different from those of Pakistan. The Jamaat leaders in Bangladesh still expect women to fulfill domestic obligations but they also acknowledge them as individuals who have 'individual' responsibilities to God and Islam. They also acknowledge Islam's support for women's right to study, work and vote. This is a tactical change in the strategy of the Jamaat in Bangladesh where the outfit has taken the shape of a political party and is looking for mass support.

On the eve of the 1996 elections there was a massive mobilisation against the Jamaat as it also coincided with 25th anniversary of independence. The secular organistaions of the country campaigned actively in favour of the 'ideals of 1971' and against those who had opposed the independence of Bangladesh. In the run-up to the elections the primary issue appeared to be the tension between the secular forces of the nation and the decidedly more Islamic direction the state had taken in the past two decades.

This movement of the secular forces helped the Awami League to come to power after the 1996 elections. The Jamaat, which had won 18 seats in 1991, could manage only three seats. There was a feeling in the party that its dismal performance was due to the mobilisation of poor women against it. The party was shunned by even the rural women who were practicing Muslims not so much because of its role during the liberation war but because of the perception that the party was opposed to their upliftment through NGO activities.

Jamaat now realises that if it wants the support of this section then it has to offer these destitute women educational and employment opportunities. So now the Jamaat is following a policy that the country's women have both material and spiritual needs. The party is now laying more emphasis on access to education and employment, ensuring sufficient food to feed their families, and a safe environment within and outside the home.

The Jamaat leaders now routinely discuss the role of the mother in Muslim society, and the privileged status of women in Islam. This is being used to counter the claims of the largely secularist NGOs operating in the country that Islam discriminates against women and the only route to progress is to discard the shackles of religion and tradition.[13]

Jamaat has tried to propagate its version of Islam among the impoverished women. Its workers discuss voting and elections in some detail with the inhabitants of slums. Jamaat is also trying to impress people by presenting an honest image which could be a great advantage in a country where political scene is charaterised by corruption under both authoritarian and democratic rule.

However, Jamaat has not been very successful in winning women over to its side. Despite being in alliance with the BNP in 2001 elections the party won only 17 seats. This was in part because the Jamaat continues to cast women in a subordinate role in society. It continues to insist on a strict form of purdah as the most important symbol of authentic Islam. It is against women working alongside men in garment factories and in NGOs. These two sectors are the largest and most visible employers of Bangladeshi women in recent decades. Jamaat's anti-women approach is revealed by its stand on family law, share in family property and its refusal to field female candidates for parliament. There are thus inherent contradictions in the Jamaat's support of democratic rights for women. As a result, women are less than enthusiastic about the Jamaat.[14]

Right-wing Media

In Bangladesh, there is also an 'alternative media' owned by the Islamists. The two well-known daily newspapers *Sangram* and *Inqilab* are part of it. They along with several Bengali weeklies and monthly magazines, promote the cause of Islam and the Muslim heritage in Bangladesh. Another daily, *Al-Mujaddidi,* has also joined this group now. A group of pro-Islamic writers regularly publish articles on the distinctive culture and history of the Muslims in Bengal and the importance of Islam in Bangladesh politics and society.

Influence of Jamaat in Administration

The reliance of the BNP on the Jamaat for support enabled the latter to wield political and administrative influence disproportionate to its political clout. This has allowed Jamaat to make big inroads into the administration. It is now using this influence for political purposes. At least five secretaries during the four-party regime were card carrying members of Jamaat.[15] Some say up to 40 per cent of the top bureaucrats have sympathies with Jamaat. Jamaat recruited a large number of agricultural officers while it was in government who are spreading Islamic law in the rural areas.

Use of Police

The police force of Bangladesh is completely politicised. They act at the behest of their political masters. The police are believed to be even acting as informants for the militants.[16] They joined hands with Islamic militants when they could not meet the challenge of left-wing extremism in northern districts of Bangladesh. The Jamaat as part of the four-party ruling coalition recruited large number of militants as sub-inspectors of police. Bangladesh intelligence agencies informed the four-party government of this but no action was taken against them. This police force is hand in glove with the Islamic militants and allowed them to operate even during the emergency rule.

The police administration allowed the Hizbut Touhid to continue its activitues in Patuakhali as it is not a 'banned organisation.' This organisation kept propagating jihad by distributing books and leaflets among villagers including school children. The organisation says that military measures are a must to establish Islam. They also stated in leaflet entitled *'Prokrito Islamer Daak'* that while people in Bangladesh were observing Islamic rules at a personal level, like namaz, Ramadan, Hajj, etc, but in the field of economics, politics, the judiciary, and other social activities they were following the rules made by men. Hence they were all "mosreqs."[17]

Similarly, a lesser known militant outfit Allahr Dal was allowed to regroup in the western part of Bangladesh and carry out its covert activities in Kushtia, Meherpur and Chuadanga. They urged people to join hands with them for establishing 'rule of Islam' in the country.[18] There are a multitude of such instances.

Use of Army

The role of army becomes important in predominantly Muslim countries of South Asia like Pakistan and Bangladesh where the army is an important institution and has the capability to displace the civilian government without great difficulty. In Bangladesh the Jamaat has been able to cultivate significant support in the army. It is generally believed that about ten per cent of the army men subscribe to the ideology of Jamaat. Ghulam Azam whose son was a major general in the army is the most powerful Jamaat leader. People recruited by Jamaat have now risen to senior positions.[19]

The Bangladesh army also has a moderate section. In fact, now those Generals are taking over who were recruited after the Liberation War. The Bangladesh army also sends one of the largest contingents to UN peacekeeping operations. That has also had a moderating influence on the armed forces because they fear that if they take over the government they would be penalised by the international community. But the army also is influenced by the political regime. Though the army knew what four-party alliance was doing the generals kept quiet in the hope of being awarded.

Use of Financial Resources

The failure of the Bangladesh state to address unemployment, poverty, environmental degradation and the political order has been seen as the most important reason for the rise of militant Islam in Bangladesh. In the immediate aftermath of the liberation war, there was deterioration on the socio-economic condition of Bangladesh. The economic crisis was compounded by political problems. The system of governance in Bangladesh is apathetic, secretive and unaccountable. Bangladesh was identified as the most corrupt country by Transparency International for three consecutive years. No wonder then, that development and aid do not reach the needy and human security is nearly non-existent in the country. Nearly half of the population in Bangladesh lives on less than a dollar a day.[20] The noted economist of Bangladesh, Abul Barkat says that 83 per cent of the population is now poor.[21]

This economic reality is perfect for the growth of radical Islam which offers a solution for spiritual as well as economic needs. The failure of the Bangladeshi state to deliver to people has created a kind of vacuum which the Islamist political parties are trying to fill. Parties like the Jamaat have a widespread social, political, economic and health network. They are trying to fulfil the responsibilities abdicated by the state. In exchange they are asking people to follow their version of Islamic ideology. Jammat is getting its funds from Islamic NGOs and donations. In the year 2005 the Islamic NGOs of Bangladesh were getting donations in excess of Taka 200 crore every year.[22] The number of local Islamic NGOs has reportedly increased significantly after a Jamaat-e-Islami leader became social welfare minister. In 1999, a Bangladesh Intelligence agency was reportedly tracking the Servants of Suffering Humanity International (SSHI) an organisation that was working to establish a Taliban style fundamentalist government in Bangladesh and was funded by bin-Laden.[23]

Besides, these the Jamaat has its own financial resources. The former Industries Minister Matiur Rahman Nizami, the Amir of the Jamaat has helped promote the growth of a Jamaat economic empire that embraces banking, insurance, trucking, pharmaceutical manufacturing, department stores, newspapers and TV stations. A study conducted by a leading Bangladeshi economist Abul Barkat estimates annual net profit of fundamentalist organisations to be about $200 million (Bd Tk 12,000 million).[24]

Recently, Jamaat has undertaken several new economic roles. Following in footsteps of Professor Yunus Jamaat has also started giving micro-credit to the people. This has been done with the objective of increasing their hold on Muslim society.

The Jamaat is helping people to get overseas jobs especially in the gulf countries through their contacts. It's a mutually beneficial relationship. The people sent by them contribute Zakat to Jamaat. This is one of the major sources of funds for the local Islamic NGOs and Qaumi madrassas that do not have government recognition. Thy also do not give details of their income and expenditure to any government body. This has acted as an incentive and the Qaumi madrassas have now sprung up across the country. Jamaat also uses them to spread its ideology.

Use of International Issues

The Jamaat and other Islamic groups in Bangladesh have adroitly used some of the international issues for their advantage. They have tried to cash in on issues such as the Israel Palestine issue, Kashmir issue, Babri Masjid, the United States support to Israel, Afghanistan, and the invasion of Iraq. The taking of a rigid stand on these issues creates a constituency for them in Bangladesh. Many of these causes are seen as those of the global Islamic community. They portray Muslims as the victims of injustice.

Political Rise of Jammat after the Restoration of Democracy

The restoration of democracy in Bangladesh in 1990 provided Jamaat with the opportunity to assert itself politically. The two mainstream political parties, the Awami League and the BNP need public support to win elections. They cannot ignore the mass appeal of Islam as a religious and cultural symbol. The prestige of Jamaat increased when the citizenship of its most prominent leaders Ghulam Azam was restored after a long and acrimonious public debate. The party also generally manages to get two dozen parliamentary seats that enables it to play the role of kingmaker. Coalition politics became the norm in Bangladesh after 1990 which allowed the Jamaat to emerge as an important political player. Coalition politics forces dominant parties to make concessions to lesser players. As the rivalry between two main political parties became more petty and personal they started conceding more to the lesser parties in exchange for support. This is why the Jamaat had a larger say in the four-party BNP led alliance.[25]

For the first time in the history of Bangladesh, the fifth parliamentary elections were held on 27 February 1991 under a neutral interim government headed by Chief Justice Shahabuddin Ahmed.[26] Since it was a transition from military rule to democracy there was no ruling party and elections were not boycotted by any political group. These elections were also generally free from violence and considered free and fair.

These elections however brought to the fore the struggle between Bengali nationalism followed by the Awami League and the Bangladeshi nationalism that the BNP was trying to propagate. The election manifesto of the Awami League pledged to restore parliamentary democracy and secularism and emphasised "Bengali nationalism." The BNP, on the other hand, put emphasis on "Bangladeshi nationalism," "absolute trust and faith in Almighty Allah," and "social and economic justice."[27] The BNP manifesto avoided any debate over the future form of government by simply pledging to provide a multi-party democracy. They also wanted voters to decide whether to shout 'Joy Bangla' or Bangladesh 'Zindabad', adopt pro- or anti-Indian posture in the task of nation-building.[28]

Political analysts had predicted a comfortable majority for the Awami League in the elections. However, when the results were announced, the BNP emerged as the single largest party with 140 seats and the Awami League could get only 88 seats. Although both the BNP and the Awami League polled nearly an equal percentage of popular votes, the number of seats won by the BNP was much higher.[29] Similarly, even with a lower percentage of the popular vote, the Jatiya Party managed to get more seats than the Jamaat. This was contrary to expectation, as it was generally believed that after the removal of Ershad from power, his party would vanish from Bangladesh politics. The party got a respectable 35 seats and Ershad himself was victorious from five seats despite being interned at the time. The results however indicated that the Jamaat was gradually consolidating its position.[30]

The Jamaat was able to win 18 seats possibly due to its last minute alliance with the BNP. This was eight more than what it had got in the 1986 election. The number of seats won by Jamaat were few but this proved useful as it enabled the BNP to get 28 of the 30 reserved seats for women, thus giving it an absolute majority in parliament.[31]

The success of the BNP was due to many factors including: the uncompromising attitude of Khaleda Zia towards Ershad and his regime; the popularity of its student wing (the Jatiyatabadi Chhatra Dal); the successful exploitation of the anti-Indian and pro-Islamic sentiment of the electorate; and the complacency of the Awami League, translated into an unplanned and poorly coordinated election campaign.[32] Khaleda proved to be a much better campaigner than Hasina, and those around her also spoke well and were in sync with the party leader.[33] The BNP also had the advantage of being funded by the ISI.[34] The former ISI Chief Asad Durrani has now admitted that they had financed Khaleda Zia during the 1991 elections. Just prior to this revelation a UAE-based daily had alleged that the ISI had given Rs 50 crores to BNP chairperson Khaleda Zia ahead of the 1991 elections which she won and formed the government. The closeness of the BNP with the ISI was always suspected but it came out in the open only recently.

The coming to power of the BNP after the 1991 elections ensured that the reversal of secularism would continue. Though, a section in the BNP was allergic to Jamaat the constant agitation of the Awami League only pushed the BNP further into the lap of the Jamaat. This was apparent in the way the government handled the agitation demanding the trial of the Jamaat chief, Ghulam Azam.

Ghulam Azam had sided with Pakistan during the liberation war. He was forced to leave the country in 1971 but sneaked back in 1978 and has continued to stay ever since without any objections. Things however, changed in 1991 when Ghulam Azam was elected 'Amir' of Jamaat-e-Islami for the fourth time and this was announced publicly. This provoked a small number of anti-Jamaatis, who were close to the five-party alliance, to set up a committee for the trial and elimination of the killers and collaborators of 1971 and the revival of the spirit of the liberation war ('Nirmul'). The committee's activities climaxed in a huge public rally on 26 March, where a 'gano adalat' (people's court) of 24 lawyers pronounced that Ghulam Azam's crimes were punishable by death.

Begum Zia's government acted in haste and filed cases of sedition against the 24 political activists who had sponsored the 'gano-adalat' at the metropolitan magistrate's court, but also put Ghulam Azam behind bars for staying 'illegally' in Bangladesh. The arrest angered the Jamaat—especially its youth brigade—and it set up a parallel body to demanding that the organisers of the 'gano adalat' be tried as 'Indian agents'. In short it was a clash of Bangladeshi nationalism with pan-Islamic fundamentalism. The violent demonstrations and sustained boycott of parliament by the opposition, forced the government to agree to trying Azam in court and withdrawing the cases against the 24 sponsors of the 'gano-adalat'.

Soon after this commotion, the Awami League paralysed Dhaka by organising a strike on 15 August, on the occasion of the 17th death anniversary of Sheikh Mujib-ur-Rahman. The party demanded the arrest and trial of the self-proclaimed killer of Mujib-Faruq Rahman who, again, had been allowed by the government not only to come back to Bangladesh (from his self-imposed exile abroad) but also to form a political party to legitimise his status. The Awami League wanted the government to repeal an indemnity ordinance—passed after Mujib's assassination—that prevented the trial of Mujib's killers.[35]

The Awami League also boycotted the budget session. This boycott put a lot of pressure on the BNP government and pushed the party into the lap of the Jamaat—the very force the Awami League claimed to be fighting. There is a large group in the BNP which is as allergic to the Jamaat as any other party. It is this group that lost its nerve when the 18 Jamaat MPs stayed back in parliament to give the government the symbolic support which it badly needed to present the annual budget. But the Jamaat also extracted its 'pound of flesh' and got Ghulam Azam released.[36] The Jamaat then fanned out into remote districts to bide its time before storming Dhaka.

In 1996 elections Jamaat won only three parliamentary seats. The election of Ghulam Azam as the party chief revived bitter memories of Pakistani military repression and the alleged collaboration of Gholam Azam and other Jamaat leaders with Pakistan in the Bengali war of independence. The Jamaat also failed to strike an alliance either with the Awami League or any other major party which further hurt the party in the 1996 general elections.[37] Women rejected it for its stand against women's rights.

After the 2001 elections, in which the BNP won a commanding mandate of 192 seats out of 300, religious parties became even more politically irrelevant. The Jamaat won 17 seats and the other BNP religious partner, the Islami Oikyo Jote (IOJ), won only two. Even with such lack lustre performances, paradoxically, the religious parties gained strength and were further emboldened. The coalition politics of Bangladesh allowed the Jamaat to have greater say in the government and the militant elements were able to attack symbols of Bangla culture with impunity as they had little to fear. Both the Jamaat and IOJ consolidated their own agenda for an Islamic state and their anti-India policy in lieu of enhancing coalition cooperation.[38]

The Jamaat has used both mainstream political parties to advance its political standing. Its alliance with the BNP has been more direct and visible, but it has also used Awami League. One can also say that it is the Awami League which occasionally sought the help from the Jamaat. The Jamaat even claims that:

> After the general elections of 1991, on behalf of Awami League, Amir Hossain Amu made an offer to Jamaat through Ali Ahsan Mohammad Mujahid, the present secretary general of Jamaat to form government

> with the help of 18 MPs of Jamaat and in return Jamaat was offered 2-3 ministries with a number of seats reserved for women MPs." Jamaat claims it refused the offer of Awami League.[39]

Islam was used by Zia-ur-Rahman to gain legitimacy and he was the one who removed the ban on religious parties which is why parties like the Jamaat have naturally found BNP much closer to them ideologically. The maturing of this relationship was seen during the government of the four-party alliance, where the Jamaat and IOJ were part of the ruling coalition. This relationship came under some stress when the term of the coalition ended in 2006. The IOJ, for a brief period, broke away from this coalition. But generally it is believed that it was a pressure tactic on the part of the IOJ to get more seats so that they could lay claim to more ministries. This strain evaporated as the election approached and these parties are now together once again.

The Awami League is generally perceived as being secular. It is alleged however that this party also did not take serious action against these Islamist groups when it was in power. In fact, some people accuse even Sheikh Mujib-ur-Rahman of not acting sternly against the Jamaat and other Islamists immediately after the liberation war. Despite Mujib's promises to ensure exemplary punishment to the collaborators involved in the murder, rape and torture, the Bangladesh Collaborators (Special Tribunals) Order 1972, issued on 24 January, of that year, had several loopholes. As a result, out of the 37, 471 cases initiated only 752 resulted in punishment—and these were ridiculously light.[40]

What was worse, on 30 Novermber 1973 Mujib suddenly proclaimed, a general amnesty for all those who were under trial and all who had been convicted, under the Bangladesh Collaborators (Special Tribunals) Order 1972. Not only that, he ordered their release within a week so that they could participate in the third Victory Day celebrations on 16 December 1973, and called upon them to participate in the rebuilding of the country.[41] Whatever, be the reason behind Mujib's decision it made these forces strong and opened Awami League to allegation by the Jamaat that it did not take legal action against them for war crimes during its two terms in office: from 1972-75 and 1996-2001.[42] The Jamaat also points out that during the mass movement for restoration of democracy in the 1980s and during the movement for a caretaker government in the 1990s, the Awami League had no difficulty in working side by side with Jamaat leaders, whom it is now accusing of war crimes.[43]

During its earlier tenure (1996-2001) the Awami League government also did not make any serious attempt to strengthen secularism in the country.

For instance, the Awami League made only a half-hearted attempt to dismantle the Vested Property Act (which had deprived Hindus of their homes and land holdings as early as 1969) towards the fag end of its regime in 2001. It's hardly surprising that this effort could not bring any relief to the minority Hindu community. Many people saw this only as a political gimmick to ensure minority votes for the Awami League. Now, it is also alleged that to appeal to the orthodox, Awami League members are publicly using religious symbols and slogans.[44]

The Awami League surprised everyone when it tied up with the Khilafat Mazlis, a radical Islamist group in January 2007. At that time the Iajuddin Ahmed led caretaker government was planning to hold elections. This not only perplexed the party rank and file it also seriously damaged their secular credentials. Some alleged that Islamists had paid huge sums of money to some Awami League leaders for this alliance. But it seems political considerations also prompted the Awami League to go for this opportunistic alliance.

The two mainstream political parties in Bangladesh get nearly the same percentage of votes. The Islamists vote share varies from four to eight per cent. Thus this vote actually gives an edge to the party they ally with. In the 2001 elections, the Awami League actually increased its vote share from 37 to just over 40 per cent. Though the BNP's vote share also increased marginally, it was able to sweep the polls because of its well-thought-out electoral alliance.[45] A cursory look at the election returns of 1996 and 2001 shows that a relatively small increase in the BNP's vote (8 per cent, perhaps half of which was the transfer of the Jamaat support) led to a 44 per cent increase in the seats won. The Awami League, despite increasing its vote (3 per cent), witnessed a 57 per cent decline in the number of seats won. A small shift in the voting pattern produces a disproportionate outcome. This is, of course, a vagary of the first-past-post voting system.[46]

It was to negate this advantage of the BNP that the Awami League probably entered into an alliance with Khilafat Mazlis. Through this alliance it wanted to attract the orthodox voters but it was a misconception on the part of the Awami League to think that it could use the Khilafat for its purposes because the Khilafat would have wanted the Awami League to share its agenda. Allying with Khilafat was like allying with the Jamaat. Top Jamaat leaders reiterate that there is no basic difference between their party and other Islamist groups.[47] They will all become one when they are sufficiently strong and parties like Awami League will be dumped.

However the Awami League realised that its alliance with the Islamists would only have helped the extremists in the long term. The Islamists and

Jamaat have no illusion about the Awami League. They deem it to be a secular party, whereas they consider BNP to be a nationalist party, which has the Bangladeshi concept. Hence they might ally with Awami League for the short term but, Islamists ultimately want an Islamic state. For the Awami League to ally with the Islamists would be like digging its own grave.

The Place of Jamaat in Bangladeshi Politics

There is no doubt that there has been a tremendous resurgence of Islamic forces in Bangladesh since the mid-1970s. But their support base is likely to remain divided between those who would follow the Jamaat and those who would vote for centrist parties that will be friendly towards Islamic forces.

The common people of Bangladesh are still reluctant to accept the Wahabi ideology of the Jamaat. Women, who have played an important role in Bangladeshi society, are especially sceptical of the Jamaat. Though the Jamaat has often tried to mislead women by trying to highlight their role as mothers in Muslim homes, the Bangladeshi women want much more than that. Hence even rural women who are more influenced by religion, they too are wary of Jamaat and consider it to be a hurdle in the way of their progress. But the Jamaat is continuing to make inroads because of its strong organisational machinery. It is luring people and bureaucrats and sometime even using force where they are in a position to do so. Most importantly, when Jamaat was in power it tried to create a system that would benefit its followers and put the others at a disadvantage. Minorities and others, of course do not have any place in their scheme of things.

The Jamaat extended its reach when it was part of the four-party alliance. It has many adherents in the civil service which despite the corruption is looked up to by the common man. It is feared that Jamaat can use this to manage votes and support.

The Jamaat is consistently working in Bangladesh to achieve its avowed objective of Islamic state. In this effort it has been supported by both military dictators as well as the democratic governments. Though in the initial phases after liberation the growth of political Islam in Bangladesh was a top down phenomenon, Islamists of Bangladesh have now come to a stage where they can sustain themselves and grow at a rapid pace.

It has also been suggested that Bangladesh's indigenous culture and society are a natural defence against extremism but unfortunately both the culture and the progressive elements of society have been under attack. The state control over the universities ensures that people in power are able to pack them with loyalists in order to indoctrinate the younger generations.[48] Dhaka

2001 Elections: Share of Votes of Top Ten Political Parties

Sl. No	*Party Name*	*Party Symbol*	*Candidate Contested*	*Seats won*	*Votes Obtained*	*% of Valid Votes Polled*
1.	Bangladesh National Party (BNP)	Sheaf of Paddy	259	193	23074714	41.4
2.	Bangladesh Awami League	Boat	300	62	22310276	40.02
3.	Islami Jatiya Oikya Front	Plough	280	14	4023962	7.22
4.	Jamaat-e-Islami Bangladesh	Scales	31	17	2385361	4.28
5.	Independent		486	6	2262045	4.06
6.	Bangladesh Jatiya Party (N-F)	Sheaf of Paddy(N-F)	7	4	521472	0.94
7.	Islami Oikya Jote	Sheaf of Paddy/Minar	6	2	312868	0.56
8.	Krisak Sramik Janata League	Gamcha	39	1	261344	0.47
9.	Jatiya Party (Monju)	(Bicycle)	140	1	243617	0.44
10.	Jatiya Party (Monju)	Flaming Touch(Mashal)	75	0	119072	0.21

Source: Bangladesh Election Commission http://www.ecs.gov.bd/English/ShareVote.php?&electionid=8&electionName=Parliament%20 Election%202001

University which was a bastion of liberal ideas has been penetrated by the Islamists. This university is known for the positive role it played during the liberation war in Bangladesh. Unfortunately, now it has large number of professors and students who believe that Islamic rule will be good for the country as democratic regimes and military dictatorships have not proved effective.[49] The influence of Islamic ideology is also visible in the media where there is an effort to present the terrorists as people fighting for just causes.[50] The Jamaat has its own newspaper and weekly publications through which it is trying to spread Islamist ideology.

The importance of Islamic parties is often underestimated on the grounds that they do not win many elections. But the number of seats won by them does not reflect the kind of influence they have on the Bangladeshi society. One reason why Jamaat has not done so well politically is because the party is not so keen on winning seats, but prefers, at this juncture, to make society more orthodox in other ways.

NOTES

1. "Introducing Jamaat-e-Islami Bangladsh," Department of Publications, Jamaat-e-Islami Bangladesh, May 1989. For a detailed study of Jamaat-e-Islami, Bangladesh please also see, Anand Kumar, "Jamaat and its Agenda of Islamic State in Bangladesh," *Strategic Analysis*, Vol. 33, No. 4, July 2009, 541–552
2. Ibid.
3. "War Crimes, Law and the Constitution," Central Publicity Department, Jamaat-e-Islami Bangladesh, February 2008, p. 6.
4. "War Crimes, Law and the Constitution," Central Publicity Department, Jamaat-e-Islami Bangladesh, February 2008, p 13.
5. "Introducing Jama'ate Islami Bangladsh," Department of Publications, Jama'ate Islami Bangladesh, May 1989.
6. Ibid.
7. Ibid.
8. Muhammad Kamaruzzaman, "Islam and Democracy," Publicity Department, Jamaat-e-Islami, Bangladesh, April 2005.
9. Ibid, p. 5.
10. Based on interview conducted during the field trip.
11. "Countering Terrorism in Bangladesh: A Strategy Paper," Bangladesh Enterprise Institute, July 2007, p. 4. Report claims that only 19 percent of those who were arrested for terrorism were drawn from Madrassas.
12. Based on interview conducted during the field trip.
13. Elora Shehabuddin, "Jamaat-i-Islami in Bangladesh: Women, Democracy and the Transformation of Islamist Politics," *Modern Asian Studies* 42, 2/3 (2008), Cambridge University Press, pp. 593-596.
14. Elora Shehabuddin, "Jamaat-i-Islami in Bangladesh: Women, Democracy and the Transformation of Islamist Politics," *Modern Asian Studies* 42, 2/3 (2008), Cambridge University Press, pp. 577-603.
15. Based on interview with a former senior government official.

16. "SP, 5 NGOs get JMB threat: Rangpur cop role questioned," The *Daily Star,* 25 November 2005, at http://www.thedailystar.net/2005/11/25/d5112501065.htm
17. "Militants preaching jihad in Patuakhali," the *Daily Star*, 19 January 2008, http://www.thedailystar.net/story.php?nid=19875
18. "Allahr Dal militants regrouping in three dists," The *Daily Star,* 26 January 2008, at http://www.thedailystar.net/story.php?nid=20635
19. Based on Interview.
20. Bangladesh profile, *BBC*, 19 January 2012, at http://www.bbc.co.uk/news/world-south-asia-12650940
21. Barkat contradicts govt figure of the poor, *The Daily Star*, October 9, 2011 at http://www.thedailystar.net/newDesign/news-details.php?nid=205792
22. "34 Islamic NGOs get over Tk 200cr from donors a year," The Daily Star, 31 August, 2005 at http://www.thedailystar.net/2005/08/31/d5083101044.htm
23. Anand Kumar, "Islamic NGOs Funding Terror in Bangladesh," Paper no. 1531, 12 September 2005, http://www.southasiaanalysis.org/papers16/paper1531.html
24. Abul Barkat, "Economics of Fundamentalism and the growth of Political Islam in Bangladesh," *Social Science Review*, The Dhaka University Studies, Part-D, volume 23, Number 2, December 2006, pp. 17-18.
25. Imtiaz Hussain, "Fundamentalism and Bangladesh: No Error, No Terror" *South Asian Survey*, Sage Publication (Los Angeles/London/New Delhi/Singapore) 14: 2 (2007): 207-229.
26. Stanley A. Kochanek, "The Rise of Interest Politics in Bangladesh," *Asian Survey*, Vol. 36, No. 7 (July, 1996), p. 705.
27. M. Rashiduzzaman, "Political Unrest and Democracy in Bangladesh," *Asian Survey*, Vol. 37, No. 3 (March, 1997), p. 259.
28. Anirudha Gupta, "Bangladesh: Democracy Dhaka-Style," *Economic and Political Weekly*, Vol. 27, No. 30 (Jul. 25, 1992), pp. 1601-1602.
29. M. Rashiduzzaman, "Political Unrest and Democracy in Bangladesh," *Asian Survey,* Vol. 37, No. 3 (March, 1997), p. 259.
30. Ibid, pp. 259-60.
31. Zillur R. Khan, Bangladesh's Experiments with Parliamentary Democracy, *Asian Survey,* Vol. 37, No. 6 (Jun., 1997), pp. 575-589.
32. Ahmed Shafiqul Huque and Muhammad A. Hakim, Elections in Bangladesh: Tools of Legitimacy, *Asian Affairs,* Vol. 19, No. 4 (Winter, 1993), pp. 248-261.
33. Craig Baxter and Syedur Rahman, "Bangladesh Votes-1991: Building Democratic Institutions," *Asian Survey,* Vol. 31, No. 8 (Aug., 1991), p. 690.
34. "Ex-ISI boss admits funding BNP," bdnews24.com, 16 March 2012 at http://www.bdnews24.com/details.php?id=220462&cid=3, also see "Ex-ISI chief admits funding BNP polls '91," The *Daily Star*, 17 March 2012 at http://www.thedailystar.net/newDesign/news-details.php?nid=226659
35. Appeasing Fundamentalists, *Economic and Political Weekly*, Vol. 27, No. 34 (Aug. 22, 1992), p. 1770.
36. Anirudha Gupta, "Bangladesh: Democracy Dhaka-Style," *Economic and Political Weekly*, Vol. 27, No. 30 (Jul. 25, 1992), pp. 1601-1602.
37. Zillur R. Khan, Bangladesh's Experiments with Parliamentary Democracy, *Asian Survey*, Vol. 37, No. 6 (June, 1997), p. 587.
38. Imtiaz Hussain, "Fundamentalism and Bangladesh : No Error, No Terror," *South Asian Survey,* SAGE Publications Los Angeles/London/New Delhi/Singapore, 14 : 2 (2007), p. 217.

39. "War Crimes, Law and the Constitution," Central Publicity Department, Jamaat-e-Islami Bangladesh, February 2008, p. 13.
40. Hiranmay Karlekar, "*Bangladesh: The Next Afghanistan*" Sage Publications, New Delhi, 2005, p. 49.
41. Ibid. p. 49.
42. "War Crimes, Law and the Constitution," Central Publicity Department, Jamaat-e-Islami Bangladesh, February 2008, p. 12.
43. Ibid. p. 12.
44. Sumit Ganguly, "*The Rise of Islamist Militancy in Bangladesh,*" Special Report, United States Institute of Peace, Washington DC, August 2006 at http://www.usip.org/pubs/specialreports/sr171.pdf.
45. G Parthasarathy, "The Return of Khaleda Zia," November 7, 2001 at http://www.rediff.com/news/2001/nov/07gp.htm
46. Proposal Summary: Poll-Level Electoral Return Map at http://www.ndibd.org/election_analysis.php
47. This was revealed in an interview with a top Jamaat leader.
48. Imtiaz Ahmed, "Role of Academics in Combating Terrorism: Can Bangladeshi Academicians make a Difference?" Paper presented at Bangladesh Institute of International and Strategic Studies, Dhaka, p. 3.
49. Based on Interview conducted during the field visit.
50. Mahfuz Ullah, "Role of Media in Combating Terrorism," Paper presented at Bangladesh Institute of International and Strategic Studies, Dhaka on 6 April, 2008.

4

Growth of Islamist Militancy in Bangladesh

Islam was adopted as the state religion of Bangladesh on 7 June 1988, as per the Eighth Amendment to the constitution during the regime of General Ershad. This paved the way into politics for parties like the Jamaat-e-Islami. This also sent a signal to many militant Islamist groups, many of whom did not believe in the democratic system, that time was also opportune for them to make their presence felt in Bangladesh. The conciliatory approach of the government towards Islamic fundamentalists emboldened them. A further fillip to militancy was provided at the end of Afghan War against the Soviets. The victory in the Afghan war not only boosted the morale of Islamists and Muslim radicals the world over it also led to the diffusion of radicalism and Islamist militancy. The jihadis who had gathered in Afghanistan were asked to return to their respective countries and work for the establishment of 'true' Islam and the Islamic system of governance.

In Bangladesh the Jamaat is the face of political Islam. But along with it a large number of other groups also emerged who did not believe in democratic system of governance. Though the Jamaat also wants Islamic state, it is willing to wait it out and work within the democratic system, the militant Islamists are impatient and want the immediate establishment of the Islamic system of governance (Sharia). These militants started attacking democratic institutions with the objective of paralysing the state.

The attacks on leftist and secular leaders started in the early 1990s. The extremists killed Ratan Sen, the president of the Khulna branch of the Communist Party of Bangladesh, on 31 July 1992. Sen had participated in the 'Tibhaga' movement of the peasantry in the pre-partition days. He had also fought in the liberation war of Bangladesh. Subsequently, Rashed Khan Menon, the lone parliament member of the left-wing Workers' Party was also targeted. This party was part of the five-party alliance that spearheaded the agitation along with Begum Khaleda Zia's Bangladesh Nationalist Party and the Awami League, and forced General Ershad to step down in December 1990.[1]

The radical groups however were especially active during the rule of four-party alliance from 2001-06. By this time the extremists had established themselves in a section of Bangladeshi society. The presence of Jamaat and the IOJ in the BNP led alliance gave the radicals a sense of immunity and most members of the BNP also had no problems with it. This was a perfect setting for the Islamist terrorism to make its entry into Bangladesh. It announced its arrival by bombing of cenema halls for screening offensive materials on 7 December 2002. The funding from the gulf countries only abetted this process.

At present there are several militant groups in Bangladesh. The important ones among them are HuJI, JMB and Hizb-ut-Tahrir apart from various other smaller groups. Rohingya refugees who live in the Cox Bazar area of Bangladesh have also joined hands with the jihadi militants. These militant groups have objectives very similar to Jamaat and want to achieve them by violent method. In fact, most often top leaders of these organisations have been associated with the Jamaat.

Harkat-ul-Jihad-al Islami Bangladesh (HuJI-B)

The formation of the Harkat-ul-Jihad-al Islami Bangladesh (HuJI-B) by a group of Afghan war veterans under the leadership of Sheikh Abdus Salam was announced at a press conference on 30 April 1992.[2] This organisation was funded by bin Laden so that Bangladesh, a moderate Islamic state could be converted into a hardline one. Mufti Abdul Hannan, who also has links with international militant groups, is the operation commander of the Bangladesh chapter of the HuJI.[3] Now both Abdus Salam and Abdul Hannan are behind bars in Bangladesh.

Terror Activities

HuJI has been active in terror activities both inside Bangladesh as well in the neighbouring countries. Inside Bangladesh it has attacked top leaders of the Awami League including Sheikh Hasina. The HuJI has built up a network across madrassas. It has organised arms training for students in hilly forested areas. They were also dispatched to Myanmar to fight on behalf of Rohingya militants against the Myanmarese army.

The HuJI is held responsible for a large number of terrorist activities in India. HuJI was suspected to be involved in serial bomb blasts that took place in a number of Indian cities. HuJI has also been engaged in terror activities in India in concert with some Pakistani groups like Lashkar-e-Taiba (LeT) and Jaish-e-Mohammed (JeM).[4]

The HuJI was banned in October 2005 after the country wide bomb blasts.[5] The US has declared it a foreign terrorist organisation. In early 2008, the caretaker government of Bangladesh contemplated taking the help of the Indian government to question two HuJI terrorists, Anisul Mursalin and Mahibbul Muttakin lodged in Tihar jail in New Delhi. These terrorists hailing from Faridpur in Bangladesh have been in jail since the Indian police arrested them at the Delhi railway station on 26 February 2006 with 3 kg of high-powered explosive RDX, two electronic detonators and two pistols. In the border meeting of BSF-BDR, on 10 October 2008 at the Dawki-Tambil border outpost in eastern Meghalaya, the BDR chief, Major General Shakil Ahmed admitted that HuJI was a threat to both Bangladesh and India.

Attempt of HuJI to Disguise its Radical Character

After the HuJI was declared to be an international terrorist organisation its leaders tried to conduct their activities under different names. They also tried to disguise the radical character of the outfit. During the rule of the four-party alliance, the HuJI leaders formed their own party the Islamic Gono Andolon. They also made deliberate attempts to keep their distance from the militant campaign of Jama'atul Mujaheedin Bangladesh of that time. [6]

The Gono Andolon was renamed Sacheton Islami Janata on 19 August 2006 following an understanding with the then government which allowed them to operate freely. The HuJI leaders attempted to register the outfit as a political party after the caretaker administration took over in January 2007. According to Kazi Azizul their political advisor: "Our goal is to run the country as per the Charter of Medina that gives equal rights to all citizens irrespective of religion and ethnicity." He also informed that they want to introduce Sharia (the body of Islamic religious law) only for the Muslims. Other religious and ethnic minorities may follow the existing law of the land and norms of their communities. The other top leaders of HuJI with Islamic Democratic Party blamed Mufti Hannan and Abdur Rouf for all the terror activities of HuJI. They tried to present Mufti Hannan as a leader of a splintered group of HuJI. They asserted that Hannan was expelled from the organisation in 1998.

They were finally successful in May 2008. Once they received the consent of the caretaker government they floated the Islamic Democratic Party (IDP) on 18 May 2008 which according to Kazi Azizul Huq also had 200 to 300 Afghan war veterans as members. According to HuJI leaders the caretaker government had given them the permission to register as a political party on the condition that the outfit will not resort to violence for its objective of imposing Sharia. It is also suspected that Directorate General of Forces Intelligence (DGFI) helped the HuJI in this endeavour while Brigadier General ATM Amin, a director of the DGFI, 'blackmailed' the Awami League president Sheikh Hasina into convincing the US government to support IDP.[7] This implies that the caretaker government was not against implementing Sharia if it was done peacefully. This approach is very similar to Jamaat's approach.

Jama'atul Mujaheedeen Bangladesh (JMB)

The Jama'atul Mujaheedin Bangladesh is a terror outfit that has been very active inside Bangladesh although the outfit has also extended its tentacles into the bordering districts of West Bengal. The origins of the outfit are a little obscure, but it is believed to have been founded in 1989 by Maulana Abdur Rahman. The Jama'atul Mujaheedin Bangladesh (JMB) came into limelight on 13 February 2003 when a series of bomb blasts took place inside a tin shed in the Chhoto Gurgola area in Dinajpur town, leaving three persons injured. Besides arms and ammunition police also recovered subscription receipts and leaflets of this group. Among the arrested were two employees of Hazrat Aayisa Siddiqa Salafia Islamia Girls Madrassah. It was also revealed that the organisation had been doing its "underground work" in the region for more than a year and eight of its activists were arrested on 20 May 2002.[8]

It is strongly suspected that the JMB became JMJB after an encounter with the police on 15 August 2003 in Joypurhat, and reports regarding its presence in 57 districts of Bangladesh were published. The JMJB Amir (chief) and spiritual leader Maulana Abdur Rahman were also earlier associated with JMB. Siddiqul Islam alias Bangla Bhai, was the operations commander of Jagrata Muslim Janata Bangladesh (JMJB).

Abdur Rahman was educated at a madrassa where he decided to start an organisation to realise his ambition of making Bangladesh an Islamic state. Rahman travelled to Pakistan and Saudi Arabia for higher studies. He also travelled to Afghanistan during the fundamentalist Taliban regime and built links with international terrorist networks.[9] He received training in the making of bombs, handling explosives and for operating sophisticated firearms in Afghanistan while fighting for the Mujahideen.[10] He himself trained the top-level leaders of JMB and his men smuggled explosives into Bangladesh. After returning to Bangladesh, Rahman took up a job as a translator of Arabic travel documents for Bangladeshi workers going to the Middle East, but that occupation was probably a cover for his real job of recruiting Islamic militants.

Muhammad Asadullah al-Galib, an Arabic language lecturer at the Rajshahi University and chief of the Ahle Hadith Andolon Bangladesh (AHAB) was also closely associated with Jama'atul Mujaheedin Bangladesh (JMB). It appears that the JMB and JMJB represented the same set of people before they decided to work under the umbrella of the Jama'atul Mujaheedin Bangladesh (JMB). Some also believe that the JMJB was the youth wing of JMB.[11]

A very close relationship existed between the AHAB chief Asadullah Al Galib and Rahman the two ideologues of Islamic revolution in Bangladesh. Galib and Rahman had similar ideas about the Islamic revolution. This relationship became stronger when both of them came into contact with the Indian Ahle Hadith Andolon leader Abdul Matin Salafi. Salafi was expelled from Bangladesh in 1988 for his militant activities but he still continued to work with AHAB leaders.

In the late 70s, Galib was detached from Jamayate Ahle Hadith which was founded in 1945. He went on to set up the Ahle Hadith Juba Shangha (AHJS). Rahman had studied in Madina University in Saudi Arabia and worked at the Saudi Arabia and Kuwait embassies in Dhaka on Galib's recommendation. Galib established AHAB in mid 90s and during this time he created a countrywide underground network to work for Rahman.

Galib and Rahman met several times in Chittagong in 1998 to discuss their plans for "revolution". They worked among the Muslim Rohingyas and Arakan militants. Rahman's followers who were involved in bomb blasts consisted of Jamaat-e-Islami, Islami Chhatra Shibir and AHJS members. The AHAB chief reportedly masterminded the militant actions in the country and the JMB acted as AHAB's operational wing and the HuJI as its training unit.

Different international extremists appeared at the Ahab conference in Rajshahi in the late 90s revealing AHAB's link with militants of Middle East and South Asia. Maulana Sheikh Abdullah Nasser Al Rahmani, wanted by the US Federal Bureau of Investigation (FBI) for his links with al-Qaeda; Maulana Abdul Wahab Khiljee of the Indian Punjab; the West Bengal Ahle Hadith leader Abdullah Salafi of Murshidabad and the editor of the Nepalese Ahle Hadith publication *'Noor-e Tawhid' Abdullah* Abdur Tawat Al Madani were some of the people who attended the conference. Galib introduced Salafi as a special guest despite his having been expelled from the country.[12]

The JMB has connections with the Pakistan-based militant group Lashkar-e-Taiba (LeT), which is also active in India. Foreigners have visited Bangladesh at different times in the name of religious activities and some of them have been training the JMB men. This was proved in July 2006 by the arrest of two Pakistani militants in Jhalakathi district, the hotbed of Islamist militancy. The Pakistanis were among nine militants detained in the district. One of the men had been living illegally in Bangladesh for the 18 years. They gave their names as Golam Sabbir of Sargodha in Pakistan Punjab and Belal Afsar. According to police, those detained said they were members of 'Dawat-e-Islami (Tablig and Dawat)' and claimed to be engaged in religious preaching.

The JMB gained notoriety after it carried out near simultaneous blasts in 63 out of 64 districts of Bangladesh on 17 August 2005. Although only two persons were killed in the explosions, these demonstrated the outfit's reach within the country. However, in subsequent years, JMB killed scores of people in a number of bomb blasts, which included two judges who were campaigning against the outfit.

In May 2004 Abdur Rahman disclosed that his outfit had 10,000 full-time and over one lakh part time active cadres. He also claimed to have set up a mosque and a madrassa in Jamalpur with financial assistance from Islamic NGOs Rabeta-e-Islam and another the 'Oytijjho Sangstha' (Kuwait-based Revival of Islamic Heritage Society). Jama'atul Mujaheedin Bangladesh is demanding the imposition of strict Islamic law in Bangladesh.

The outfit suffered a major blow when six of its top leaders were executed on 30 March 2007.[13] Among those executed were its founder chief Sheikh Abdur Rahman and second in command Siddiqul Islam Bangla Bhai. Since then the outfit has been trying to regroup. Its cadres get arrested at regular interval. The outfit is presently headed by Saidur Rahman who was arrested in Dhaka on 26 May 2010 after being pursued for three years.

According to the present JMB Chief Saidur Rahman the group still has around 400 full-time members and 50,000 supporters across the country.[14] It has a strong military wing that is capable of launching devastating attacks and also has a huge cache explosives, home made bombs and grenades.

Another JMB operative, Abu Bakker Sodium alias Shill, who was also arrested along with Saidur Rahman, has revealed that some of the female operatives of the group are trained in the use of grenades. The outfit at one time planned to carry out attacks in Dhaka city on a limited scale with the objective of signalling re-emergence of the group and to attract new recruits.

Presence of JMB in the Bordering Districts of West Bengal

The JMB has now expanded its operations within India and the outfit has a significant presence in West Bengal especially in districts bordering Bangladesh. The arrested JMB chief, Saidur Rahman disclosed that the outfit has been active in three border districts of West Bengal. When pressure intensified on one of the top leaders of the outfit, Sahel Mahfuz, who is the member of the JMB's highest policy making body the Majlish-e-Shura, he went underground in India. JMB has established three cells in the Malda, Nadia and Murshidabad districts of West Bengal with 100 fulltime operatives.[15] These cells are being used to smuggle explosives and weapons into Bangladesh. Rahman also disclosed that the JMB was running seven madrassas in these districts where it has nearly 10,000 sympathisers.

Though the Bangladesh government under Sheikh Hasina has been acting against the JMB, and has arrested a number of its top leaders, the outfit remains a threat.[16]

Hizb-ut-Tahrir

The Hizb-ut-Tahrir (Party of Liberation) is an Islamist organisation that has a presence in a number of countries. In Bangladesh the outfit has been active for the past eight years and is headed by Professor Mohiuddin Ahmed.[17] Hizb-ut-Tahrir has the goal of unifying all Muslim countries as a caliphate governed by Islamic law. It was banned in Bangladesh in October 2009 but is known to have continued its activities secretly.

Hizb-ut-Tahrir has been banned in at least 20 countries. In Bangladesh it topped a government list of about 10 groups suspected of plotting subversive acts in the country. It has been active lately in universities and the government is worried about its increasing influence among students.

Nearly 40 members of the organisation were arrested in 2009 after they were alleged to have distributed leaflets in support of a mutiny by border guards in which over 50 army officers were killed.

The government in Bangladesh fears that the Hizb-ut-Tahrir poses a threat to peace. The outfit also has a following among middle and lower rung military officials. It was involved in the army coup against the Sheikh Hasina government in which certain BNP and Jamaat leaders were also suspected to be involved. The Jamaat, which collaborated with the Pakistan army in 1971, is desperate to topple the Hasina government as it tightens the noose around the party by fast-tracking the trials of its leaders facing charges of war crimes.

Links of Jamaat with Militant Outfits

The Jamaat has always provided ideological base to groups who adopted violent methods to achieve the objective of establishing an Islamic state in Bangladesh. Despite its claims of being a 'moderate Islamic party' there is no doubt about it's radical character. Jamaat itself has used violent methods in the past. The Jamaat as a party fought against its own people during the liberation war and committed the worst crimes against humanity during this period. The Sheikh Hasina government has started the process of holding trials for war crimes after a gap of nearly 40 years.

The Jamaat has been careful not to use violent methods after their return from Pakistan facilitated by the BNP and military. It has tried to achieve its objective by taking the help of various other outfits because it does not want to lose its hard won acceptance in Bangladesh society. The pro-liberation people of Bangladesh have still not forgotten the dastardly acts committed by the Jamaat during the liberation war.

The student wing of the Jamaat—the Islami Chhatra Shibir (ICS)—is regularly involved in violence in various university campuses of Bangladesh. Though the Jamaat tries to distance itself from the Shibir, there are no doubts regarding its links with the organisation. The ICS leaders often become leaders of Jamaat-e-Islami once they leave university. The Jamaat has also its affiliates among the university teachers.

Jamaat has close relationships with the Islamist militant outfits of Bangladesh. In the wake of countrywide bomb blasts of 2005, the authorities arrested seven members of the Jama'atul Mujaheedin Bangladesh. All had either been members of the Jamaat or the Islami Chhatra Shibir.[18] When the former director of Islamic Academy Maulana Fariduddin Masud was detained for his suspected links with militants he told a Dhaka court that stunning facts would emerge if the law enforcers interrogated the then industries minister and the Jamaat Amir Matiur Rahman Nizami.

Even Abdur Rahman at his Sylhet hideout had a number of books on jihad and Islamic revolution, some of which were authored by the Jamaat-e-Islami founder Abul-Ala-Moududi and its former Amir Ghulam Azam. Some of the books which were recovered but not mentioned in the seizure list of police were: Moududi's *'Shantipath'*, Ghulam Azam's *'Jibanta Namaj'* and *'Allahr Ain O Sotloker Shashon'*. Although Rahman is known in Bangladesh and abroad as the chief of the Jama'atul Mujaheedin Bangladesh, he is a former activist of Jamaat. His father Abdullah ibne Fazal was a member of Jamiatul Ahle Hadith, which is now led by the arrested Rajshahi university teacher Asadullah al Galib. Fazal is accused of collaborating with the occupation Pakistani forces during the liberation war in 1971. Besides this literature on jihad, two of the four bank chequebooks found in the JMB chief Abdur Rahman's hideout belonged to Saidur Rahman.[19]

Police investigation in Bangladesh indicated that the Jhalakathi bomber and his family members had close links with Jamaat-e-Islami. He was also an activist of Islami Chhatra Shibir. The close relationship between Jamaat and JMB was further confirmed with the arrest of Maulana Saidur Rahman, a former Habiganj Jamaat-e-Islami Amir. He was involved in the Islami Chhatra Shibir from 1977 and was the president of the Moulvibazar unit of the Shibir between 1978 and 1980. In 1981, Saidur was given the charge of both Habiganj and Moulvibazar districts. In 1983, he became the Amir of the Habiganj unit of the Jamaat. He also became a member of the highest policy making body of the Jamaat, the Majlish-e-Shura. Saidur claims that he assumed the leadership of JMB as per the directive of the Jamaat Chief Matiur Rahman Nizami.

The law enforcement agencies have now also arrested the JMB's acting chief Anwar Alam Khoka alias Bhagne Shahid alias Nazmul from Bogra district. The JMB high command had appointed Shahid to the top post after the arrest of Saidur Rahman. According to Bangladesh police, Nazmul was a member of the Islami Chhatra Shibir (student wing of Jamaat) until he joined JMB in 1998. In 2001, he became a full-time member. He also became a member of the JMB's Majlish-e-Shura when it was reconstituted following the arrest of Sheikh Abdur Rahman.

The intelligentsia in Bangladesh believes that there is no difference between Jama'atul Mujaheedin Bangladesh (JMB) and the Jamaat-e-Islami. They also allege that Jamaat created the militants like Sheikh Abdur Rahman and Bangla Bhai with a view to use them for political purposes.

The Islamic parties which were part of the four-party coalition government denied any links between the government and the militant groups but confirmed that they shared the objective of the extremists to introduce the Islamic legal code or Sharia law by replacing the present legal system. The government's persistent denial of any extremist threat seemed to have been motivated largely by a desire to protect Bangladesh's international image. Whenever the media reported the rise of militant groups, Dhaka complained vociferously that the reports were damaging the country's reputation. The Jamaat MP and cabinet minister, Matiur Rahman Nizami, alleged that some journalists were guilty of "information terrorism" and "tainting the image of the country."[20]

When the six militant leaders were executed by the caretaker government, which confirmed the existence of terror groups, the Jamaat-e-Islami Amir Matiur Rahman Nizami took an interesting stand. He said that militants had killed people and engaged in criminal activities in the name of Islam, which harmed the politics of his party because their agenda is to silently ensure the Islamisation of Bangladesh. These statements were also meant to keep the law-enforcers at bay.

Link with the BNP

The extremist groups now also have links with one of the mainstream political parties, the BNP. The operations commander of the HuJI, Mufti Abdul Hannan, was arrested by the Rapid Action Battalion (RAB) of Bangladesh on 1 October 2005 on charges of sedition. He is also the prime accused in the plot to assassinate the then prime minister, Sheikh Hasina in Kotalipara in Gopalganj on 20 July 2000. Though Hannan claimed that the cases filed against him were politically motivated, he confessed that he had planted the 76-kg bomb at Kotalipara on 20 July 2000.

At the RAB office in Dhaka, Hannan disclosed that he had been staying in the country because the former home minister and later the commerce minister, Altaf Hossain Choudhury, had reassured him of his safety. He also added that Altaf could not do much for him because he had since been made commerce minister. He also revealed that the editor of monthly *Madina* Maulana Mohiuddin played the role of mediator between him and the home minister.[21] The state minister for water Gautam Chakraborty and president of BNP Gopalganj district unit had recommended mercy for Hannan.

Though the JMB and JMJB had expanded their network far and wide in Bangladesh because of the alleged political patronage of a section of the four-party alliance government they were especially strong in the northern districts of Bangladesh. A BNP lawmaker, Abu Hena who represented the Rajshahi district had accused a section of government high-ups of supporting the vigilantism of the Siddiqul Islam alias Bangla Bhai led JMJB and JMB. He had named the telecommunications minister Aminul Haque and two ministers of the ruling alliance partner Jamaat-e-Islami as patrons of the militants. But instead of taking any action against the accused, the BNP leadership chose to expel Hena from the party.

The other leaders who were allegedly involved in the militant activities were the then deputy minister for land Ruhul Quddus Talukdar Dulu and the then BNP lawmakers Nadim Mostafa and Mizanur Rahman Minu. These allegations were made by the state minister for housing and public works Alamgir Kabir during a local party meeting in Naogaon.

Political parties that participated in Khaleda Zia's (then prime minister) national dialogue in December 2005 to find ways to combat militancy had recommended instituting a judicial commission to enquire into the allegation of involvement of BNP leaders in supporting militancy. They also suggested that those within the government and the administration who are suspected of having links with militants should resign to ensure a fair investigation. But the government took no action.[22]

The second caretaker government headed by Fakharuddin Ahmed acknowledged the existence of Islamic militant organisations in the country and their link with some political parties.[23]

Political Support to Militancy

The militant organisations were not only having links with the BNP and Jamaat they were also getting their active political support during the four-party regime. Political support for militants did not allow the law enforcement agencies to do their work properly and provided immunity to the militants. Bangladesh intelligence agencies hinted at the involvement of the Jamaat and its student wing the ICS in the 17 August blasts. But they could not act against them because of the political pressure. Policemen were instructed not to harass leaders and activists of the Jamaat-Shibir and the AHAB chief Asadullah Galib and his followers.

The government's policy of arresting and releasing militants created further problems for the law enforcers. The security agencies alleged that many on the 'not-to-be harassed' list that the home ministry sent to Gaibandha and other northern districts were in fact involved with the militant groups.

For instance, police officials were instructed not to arrest Lutfor Rahman of the Bagmara upazila in Rajshahi. Lutfor, a college teacher was adviser to the militant kingpin Bangla Bhai. He had been with the Jamaat before joining hands with Bangla Bhai's JMJB. Lutfor had gone underground after the government banned JMJB on 23 February. However, after police received instructions not to harass him, he soon resurfaced in the area.

The religious parties that were member of the four-party alliance recruited militants even among the police sub-inspectors. The government was informed of the presence of extremist elements among the law enforcement agencies by the Bangladeshi intelligence agencies. They specifically called for action against one such militant cop who hailed from Bogra's Shariakandi, and was posted at the Sarda Police Academy.[24] But nothing was done.

Links with the Army

Some army men have also been found to be training Islamic militants. The Bangladesh police arrested Obaidullah Sumon with four kilograms of powder explosives, 50 detonators and 12 packets of power gel in Guduigram village of Nikli sub-district in Kishoreganj on 14 September 2005. Sumon during interrogation revealed that some of the JMB cadres were trained by a retired lance corporal of the army Harun-ur-Rashid and retired honorary army captain Mohiuddin in the making and detonating of bombs. This led to the arrest of Harun from Monipur area of Dhaka on 20 September by a team of the Detective Branch (DB) of the police.[25]

Harun, who had retired from army in 1998, confessed that he had trained the JMB cadres in bomb-making and operation techniques. He also named eight other serving defence personnel who were training the JMB bomb squads. He further revealed that JMB had recruited more than a 100 retired army men and disclosed the identities of more than 50 ex-army men. The drive to recruit non-commissioned army personnel was begun by Siddiqul Islam alias Bangla Bhai, around three years ago to strengthen the military wing of the outfit.

Following Harun's confession the military intelligence on 22 September 2005 launched their own enquiry coordinated by the Directorate General of Forces Intelligence (DGFI). The enquiry found no evidence of any links between retired and serving army personnel with the JMB. The army headquarters on 28 September said newspaper reports about the involvement of Harun-ur-Rashid and other retired and serving army men in the August 17 bomb blasts were all a fiction. It termed these reports "totally fabricated, imaginative and baseless."[26]

It also accused a certain section of the people of trying to create panic by publishing concocted stories of militant infiltration into the army and undermining the image of the army and the country.

Earlier, police in Chapainawabganj had found a military manual while arresting JMB leader Mohabbat Ali at Gomostapur.[27]

Attacks on Democratic Institutions

The most serious threat posed by the Islamist groups is to the democratic polity of Bangladesh. Though democracy in Bangladesh may not be ideal, it is still a far better alternative than a Taliban ruled state or a military dictatorship as in some pre-dominantly Muslim countries. Almost all Islamist groups are unanimous in wanting Islamic rule for Bangladesh. They only differ with regard to the means for achieving this. The Jamaat, for instance, talks of a peaceful transition to Islamic rule, whereas some of the terror outfits prefer a violent transition to Islamic rule.[28]

Interestingly, the Jamaat is against military rule and favours democracy. This is not for the love of democracy, but the outfit believes it would be far easier for it to have an Islamic state under a democratic system. It was actively involved in the movement against military rule and in support of the restoration of democracy. It was disappointed when Ershad declared Islam as the state religion in 1988 rather than declare Bangladesh to be an Islamic state. The Jamaat also played an important part in the movement for the Thirteenth Amendment. This amendment ensured that all future elections would be preceded by three months under a 'neutral caretaker government' headed by a retired chief justice.

The Jamaat has contested all four elections held in 1991, 1996, 2001 and 2008. Though the party has not been able to make an effective bid for national power, the number of seats gained by Jamaat has allowed it to become an important player in the national politics of Bangladesh. Jamaat leaders in Bangladesh maintain that the party was in no hurry to win elections and they are quite prepared to wait until the population is ready for an Islamic state. This is unlike other extremist organisations who have taken to violence.

The militant Islamist organisations of Bangladesh however do not want to wait for a Islamic state. They are targeting democratic institutions in the country so that the democratic set up is paralysed. The near-simultaneous bomb attacks by the JMB across Bangladesh on 17 August 2005 targeted government establishments, mainly the offices of local district administrations and the courts. Its cadres distributed leaflets which asked the government to introduce Islamic law or face the JMB offensive. In the leaflets, the militants also asked the bureaucrats and judges to cease doing their administrative and judicial duties and stop enforcing evil laws of democracy and the constitution.

The courts and the judges were targeted once again in another series of bomb blasts in Chandpur, Chittagong and Lakshmipur on 3 October 2005.[29] Yet another bomb attack was carried out in the same month on 18 October targeting a judge, Biplop Goswami, in Sylhet.

The violent activities of JMB reduced as the SAARC summit approached. The Bangladeshi intelligence agencies were of the view that militants had decided not to strike during the SAARC summit. But immediately after the summit, the JMB struck again killing two senior assistant judges and wounding three others in a suicide bomb attack in Jhalakathi on 14 November 2005. The slain judges were Shaheed Sohel Ahmed, senior assistant judge of Nalchhiti sub-district, and Jagannath Pandey, senior assistant judge of the Sadar sub-district. The attack on the very next day after the summit ended indicated that Islamists were perfectly capable of carrying out such attacks even when the summit was on.

The militant, Iftekhar Hasan Al Mamun alias Mamun Ali involved in Jhalakathi bomb attack was held by the locals and turned in to police. He confessed to being a member of the JMB suicide squad. A handwritten leaflet seized from him said, "We don't want Taguti (non-Islamic) law, let Quranic law be introduced. Law framed by humans cannot continue and only the laws of Allah will prevail."[30]

Some Other Cases Where Threats Were Issued to Judges

- In a handwritten letter on 9 November 2005 the JMB threatened to liquidate speedy trial tribunal Judge Samad in Khulna. The letter said: "The JMB does not believe in laws formulated by humans; those who conduct court proceedings by these laws would be killed for the sake of Islam."
- An unknown Islamist outfit, Islami Ranojoddha threatened to kill all the judges in Noakhali including Deputy Commissioner (DC) Shahadat Hossain Majumadar. A threat letter was sent to the DC office on 13 November 2005. It vowed to fight unto death to establish Islamic rule in the country.
- In separate incidents on 15 November 2005 the JMB threatened to blow up the Patuakhali Judge Court; and in a booklet sent by mail to the Rangamati municipality chairman urged the Muslims to establish Quranic Ayeen (Islamic Law) in Bangladesh. The letter also claimed that the outfit has a training camp at Baufal and named Asadullah Galib as its leader and Abdur Rahman as its guru. The booklet sent to Municipality Chairman Habibur Rahman by the JMJB urged the people of Bangladesh to celebrate independence day on August 14 terming 26 March 1971 as ' separation day'. It also warned that only Mohammad Ali Jinnah should be honoured as 'father of the nation."
- The JMB on 16 November sent a 'warning letter' to Sub Judge Karim, threatening to blow him to bits if he did not conduct his court proceedings according to Sharia.
- On 16 November 2005 it asked two judges—Senior Assistant Judge Tarik and Assistant Judge Kabir—in Rajshahi district to resign if they want to escape death.

- Anonymous callers on 16 November threatened UNO Sarkar and AC Biswas in Bhola that they will be killed and their offices blown up.
- Militants on 17 November 2005 threatened to bury the law minister alive in Companiganj, Noakhali while in Rajshahi, the Jama'atul Mujaheedin Bangladesh threatened to blow up the prison if its detained cadres are not freed within 12 days starting from 20 November.
- A Senior Assistant Judge of Jhalakathi MA Awal, who narrowly escaped death on 14 November, received death threats on 20 November while an anonymous caller claiming to be a JMB operative threatened to blow up Chittagong Railway Station.
- A man identifying himself as a JMB cadre on 20 November asked Senior Assistant Judge Umme Kulsum of Chittagong to conduct trials as per Islamic laws.
- The JMB on 21 November threatened to blow up the main government offices, courts and all liberation war memorials in Rangamati if "the law of Allah is not introduced and the Martyred Intellectuals Day or the Victory Day is observed." The JMB's policymaking body Majlish-e-Shura also asked its suicide squad members to fight to death to eliminate those blocking their way and to continue striking the government offices and courts.
- The JMB on 21 November 2005 announced its intentions to blow up the Tangail Press Club, the Judge Court and the DC's office in Habiganj, and threatened to kill journalists in Tangail and the executive engineer of the Sirajganj municipality.
- JMB operatives on 22 November 2005 sent letters to two judges in Munshiganj, threatening to kill them and their families.
- The JMB suicide squad on 24 November 2005 threatened to kill the Netrakona superintendent of police (SP) Ali Hossen Fakir along with his family members as he had submitted a charge sheet against the cadres of the militant outfit and sought remand of two JMB cadres—Kawser Alam Sumon and Amanullah alias Sanaullah.

Reasons for the Militants' Targeting of the Judiciary

The Islamic militants who attacked judges have little respect for the judicial system in Bangladesh. As the courts are spread all over the country, it is easier for them to attack the judges in their courtrooms. Moreover, the Islamists consider the judiciary as the most obvious barrier to the establishment of Islamic law. Without an effective judiciary no state can run. The militants believe that once the judiciary is destroyed or rendered ineffective their purpose of sabotaging the entire system of government will be fulfilled. Militants also believe that once the existing laws are rendered ineffective stopped, people will go to the persons who want to implement Sharia law for seeking justice instead of the courts. The militant cadres are also inspired by the example of the Taliban in Afghanistan who they had attempted to destroy the established judiciary before capturing power.

The Jamaat as part of the four-party coalition functioning in a democratic framework also took several measures for the ultimate establishment of Islamic rule in the country. The Jamaat chose ministries like Industry, agriculture and social welfare to increase its following in the country. The agriculture ministry recruited agricultural officers who work at the grassroots level to spread Islamic law. The Jamaat controlled distribution of fertilisers, allotting agencies only to its followers. It also controlled orphanages as part of social development ministry. The Jamaat it appeared wants to subvert the democratic polity from within, whereas its extremist partners are doing it from outside the government and political sphere.

Attack on NGOs

As part of their attack on democratic and progressive institutions, the Islamist militants started attacking NGOs in Bangladesh. In the first few months of the year 2005 they bombed the offices of some of the leading local as well as international NGOs in the country. This not only disrupted the functioning of organisations engaged in developmental work , it also made the workers of these organisations fear for their safety and security. In Bangladesh, most government institutions are ridden with rampant corruption. In such an environment however, some commendable work has been done by some NGOs. The Islamists targeted these organisations with the objective of paralysing them.

NGOs in Bangladesh are engaged in poverty alleviation, literacy programmes and the empowerment of women through micro-credit schemes. The micro-credit schemes implemented in Bangladesh with the help of several NGOs have been hugely successful. These are a model for micro-credit scheme across the world. The Bangladesh Rural Advancement Committee (BRAC), the country's largest NGO, has been at the forefront of the country's fight against poverty. Another prominent NGO, the Grameen Bank is known worldwide for its pioneering work of giving small loans to the poor to help them set up businesses.

But unfortunately, success of these organisations also earned them the wrath of militants who want to take society in a different direction. This has prompted a series of attacks on the offices of these organisations which are as follows:

- Extremists attacked the Mohimaganj BRAC office in Gaibandha district on 10 February 2005 injuring three of its employees in two powerful bomb blasts. The JMB active in Shaghata and surrounding areas was suspected to be involved in the attack.
- Another attack took place on the BRAC office in Kalai upazila sadar in the Joypurhat district on 13 February 2005. In this attack two persons were killed.
- A similar attack was made on the BRAC office in Porsha, in Naogaon district on 15 February severely injuring four of the office staff.
- On the same day, three powerful hand grenades were recovered from the premises of a BRAC office in Rangpur.
- Three bombs were hurled on 16 February at the Grameen Bank branch at Nabagram village in Ullapara sub-district of Sirajganj district, leaving two bank employees critically hurt.
- The office of an international NGO, 'Caritas' was bombed in northern Dinajpur on March 1.

These incidents have put Bangladesh in the category of Afghanistan and Iraq where humanitarian and development organisations have been targeted. The targeting of these organisations and their workers gives the terrorists the additional satisfaction of retaliating against the West. Besides, NGOs are soft targets. These attacks created terror among the workers of the NGOs in Bangladesh.

These bomb attacks were also condemned by the Awami League and its chief Sheikh Hasina who were in the opposition at that time. She accused the four-party alliance government of protecting and patronising the attackers.

The BNP led coalition was critical of the NGOs from the very beginning. It had planned to gain control over them by trying to enact the Foreign Donations (Voluntary Activities) Regulation (Amendment) Act, 2004. This bill was designed to give government authority to remove the NGO heads and other officials. The government also wanted to prohibit involvement of NGO staff in political activities. It defined the term "political activity" in such a way that many programmes of the NGOs like the campaign for good governance, voter education, fight against corruption, advocacy, policy analysis, women's empowerment and legal aid could easily linked to politics in order to punish these organisations. However, this proposed Act had to be withdrawn because of pressure from donors and protests by the NGO community.

But the government was successful in weakening the NGOs by splitting Association of Development Agencies in Bangladesh (ADAB).[31] It created the Federation of NGOs in Bangladesh (FNB) which was generally hostile to ADAB. The government also tried to restrict the activities of some of the leading NGOs like Proshika. It restricted their funding and detained some of their senior staff including Kazi Faruq, the executive director of Proshika. These steps stalled developmental activities and made millions suffer. But the government was not bothered as long as its political aims were served. It in fact encouraged extremists by allowing them to go scot-free. Probably the government wanted to use these extremists to cow down the NGO community in Bangladesh.

There is enough evidence to prove beyond doubt that Islamist extremists were involved in attack on the NGOs.[32] Some of them were:

- A JMJB operative, Shafiqullah, who was arrested from Chaksadu village of Gabtali sub-district on 16 January 2005 disclosed to police that its cadres had plans to undertake bomb attacks on movie theatres all over the country. He also admitted that JMJB has been responsible for a number of bomb attacks on NGOs. He said the JMJB bomb squad would continue attacks on NGOs like BRAC and Caritas and cultural activities that they consider as being anti-Islamic until such time that an Islamic revolution takes place in the country.
- Twelve JMB militants were arrested from a mosque in Natore, on 1 February 2005. The arrested militants told the police that JMJB had plans to carry on attacks on the NGOs and they were undergoing training in preparation for attacks against NGOs. One of the militant said:

  We were jogging inside the mosque to train ourselves both mentally and physically against NGOs...once upon a time the East India Company captured our country in the name of business; NGOs are the new form of the company. They are patronising anti-Islamic activities and taking people away from religion. We must prepare ourselves both physically and mentally to face them.

  The leader of these militants, Forman Ali, said that they hate NGOs, as "they are spoiling our women and plotting to control our country."[33]
- The police arrested four militants—Mohbul Hossain Mahabub, Amanullah, Mamunur Rashid Mamun and Asir Uddin Kenu—while training at the Kalibari Mosque in Thakurgaon on 18 February. These militants revealed that they were followers of Galib, Salafi and Abdur Rahman. They also disclosed that their leaders while addressing at

different mosques in Dinajpur and Thakurgaon on several occasion asked them to attack NGOs, as a part of jihad. They told the police that they had joined this jihad because they were motivated by the leaders. They also admitted that they were carrying out anti-NGO propaganda at the behest of Bangla Bhai and Dr Asadullah Galib of Rajshahi University.

These attacks along with other incidents of political violence raised international concerns and under donor pressure, the government banned the JMJB and the JMB on 23 February 2005. But no serious steps were taken to check the activities of these organisations and only some local level activists were arrested.

The government arrested Asadullah Galib along with three of his associates on 23 February 2005. They were shown arrested for murder, bomb attacks, and for robbing various NGO offices in the four districts of Bogra, Gopalganj, Naogaon, and Sirajganj. The law enforcement agencies were sure of Galib's links with JMJB and JMB. He was also suspected to be involved in militant activities.

Four-party Coalition Remained Defiant Despite International Concern

The growing Islamist militancy in Bangladesh caused concern in the international community especially the US and Britain.[34] Though the donors of Bangladesh managed to put some pressure on the government to contain rising Islamic extremism the leaders of four-party ruling coalition remained hostile to them. Khaleda Zia even went on to defend Islamists in the parliament.[35]

The UK was concerned as growing extremism in Bangladesh started affecting its expatriate Bangladeshi community.[36] It was also concerned because some of its citizens were travelling to Bangladesh to train in terror techniques.[37] This concern increased when a former British high commissioner was attacked while visiting the Shah Jalal Shrine in Sylhet.

The Americans however kept treating Jamaat as a normal political party because they were training their leaders in intra and inter party democracy and as leaders.[38] Jamaat leaders were seen at American embassy parties and even visited the state department. According to some the Jamaat had used threats to get American acceptance. Their leaders had told the Americans that if their party was banned then all their cadres would go underground and form terrorist organisations like HuJI or JMB[39] creating a bigger problem for them.

The US understanding of extremism in Bangladesh was flawed. It was impossible to deal with extremism in Bangladesh while assuming Jamaat to be a normal political party. The Jamaat is a party which is operating under democratic system of government to achieve undemocratic objectives. Their objective is same as the objective of Taliban. Only the means adopted is different. But that is for strategic reasons. They know that if they become too ambitious too soon then there will be resistance from domestic political parties as well as international community. They are willing to wait for the opportune time.

The four party alliance government dropped cases against the Islamist leaders and activists and for a while it appeared that Bangladesh was heading for an Islamic takeover. Fortunately, this onward march has been stalled by the developments in last couple of years.

NOTES

1. Appeasing Fundamentalists, *Economic and Political Weekly*, Vol. 27, No. 34 (Aug. 22, 1992), p. 1770
2. "Aug 21 Grenade Attack: HuJI founder Salam held," *The Daily Star*, 3 November 2009 at http://www.thedailystar.net/newDesign/news-details.php?nid=112432
3. "HuJI boss Hannan admits to Aug 21 grenade attack," *The Daily Star*, 2 November 2007 at http://www.thedailystar.net/newDesign/news-details.php?nid=9929
4. "HuJI, LeT joining hands rattles security agencies," *The Times of India*, 1 November 2008 at http://articles.timesofindia.indiatimes.com/2008-11-01/india/27943613_1_huji-men-asif-reza-commando-force-huji-members , also see Lashkar funding HuJI operations from Bangladesh, PTI, MSN news, 12 August 2009 at http://news.in.msn.com/national/article.aspx?cp-documentid=3131123
5. "Harkatul Jihad banned at last: Govt terms it 'a terrorist outfit'," *The Daily Star*, 18 October 2005 at http://www.thedailystar.net/2005/10/18/d5101801033.htm
6. "HuJI leaders float party with govt nod: US citizen helped it get 'int'l support'," *The Daily Star*, 29 September 2008 at http://www.thedailystar.net/newDesign/news-details.php?nid=57036
7. Reaz Ahmad and Shakhawat Liton, "DGFI became militants' buddy: Amin tried to blackmail Hasina," *The Daily Star*, 16 September 2011 at http://www.thedailystar.net/newDesign/news-details.php?nid=202700
8. Anand Kumar, "Bangladesh: New Destination for Radical Islamists," *South Asia Analysis Group*, Paper No. 1273, 1 March 2005 at http://www.southasiaanalysis.org/%5Cpapers13%5Cpaper1273.html
9. "Bangladesh's most-wanted Islamic militant surrenders," *monsterandcrtics.com*, *South Asia News*, Mar 2, 2006, at http://news.monstersandcritics.com/southasia/news/article_1134057.php/Bangladesh_s_most-wanted_Islamic_militant_surrenders
10. Julfikar Ali Manik and Shamim Ashraf, "Rahman had training on arms in Afghanistan: He taught top JMB men in bomb making," *The Daily Star*, 6 March 2006 at http://www.thedailystar.net/2006/03/06/d6030601011.htm
11. "Jamaat- ul-Mujahideen Bangladesh (JMB) (Bangladesh), GROUPS—ASIA—ACTIVE,"

Jane's at http://articles.janes.com/articles/Janes-World-Insurgency-and-Terrorism/Jamaat-ul-Mujahideen-Bangladesh-JMB-Bangladesh.html
12. "Galib, Rahman on same boat of 'revolution': Observe investigators," *The Daily Star*, 5 March 2006 at http://www.thedailystar.net/2006/03/05/d60305011410.htm
13. Julfikar Ali Manik and Shariful Islam, Six JMB militants hanged, *The Daily Star*, 31 March 2007 at http://www.thedailystar.net/2007/03/31/d7033101011.htm
14. Anand Kumar, JMB Remains the Fountainhead of Terror in Bangladesh, *IDSA Comment*, 22 July 2010 at http://www.idsa.in/idsacomments/JMBRemainstheFountainheadofTerrorinBangladesh_akumar_220710
15. 'Bangladeshi militant group operates in 3 Bengal districts', *The Indian Express*, 29 May 2010 at http://www.indianexpress.com/news/bangladeshi-militant-group-operates-in-3-be/626406/
16. JMB active despite arrest of top brass: Law enforcers fear backlash, *The Daily Star,* 17 August 2010 at http://www.thedailystar.net/newDesign/news-details.php?nid=151076
17. "Bangladesh Islamist group banned," *BBC News*, 23 October 2009 at http://news.bbc.co.uk/2/hi/8321329.stm
18. Sumit Ganguly, "*The Rise of Islamist Militancy in Bangladesh*," Special Report, United States Institute of Peace, Washington DC, August 2006 at http://www.usip.org/pubs/specialreports/sr171.pdf
19. Anand Kumar, Crackdown on Terror in Bangladesh: Will it Root Out the Menace?" Paper no. 1725, http://www.southasiaanalysis.org/papers18/paper1725.html
20. Geoffrey York, "To leaders of Bangladesh, terrorism is a foreign worry: Even officials who have been threatened deny groups have wide, domestic support," *Globe and Mail*, Toronto, 29 March 2006,
21. "Mufti Hannan captured: Militant kingpin tells of Altaf's assurance of 'no fear'" *The Daily Star*, 2 October 2005 at http://thedailystar.net/2005/10/02/d5100201011.htm
22. Shakhawat Liton, Political patrons need to be caught: Stress security experts, *The Daily Star,* 3 March 2006 at http://www.thedailystar.net/2006/03/03/d6030301033.htm
23. "Militant groups patronised by some parties: Says home secretary," *The Daily Star,* 29 February 2008, at http://www.thedailystar.net/story.php?nid=25461
24. "Intelligence fears more bomb attacks," *The Daily Star*, 30 September 2005 at http://www.thedailystar.net/2005/09/30/d50930012518.htm
25. Anand Kumar, "Connivance of State and Security Agencies in August-17 Bomb-blasts of Bangladesh," *South Asia Analysis Group*, Paper no. 1570, 10 October 2005 at http://www.southasiaanalysis.org/%5Cpapers16%5Cpaper1570.html
26. News reports on army men's links a fiction: Says ISPR on Aug 17 blasts, *The Daily Star,* 29 September 2005 at http://www.thedailystar.net/2005/09/29/d5092901129.htm
27. Anand Kumar, "Connivance of State and Security Agencies in August-17 Bomb-blasts of Bangladesh," *South Asia Analysis Group*, Paper no. 1570, 10 October, 2005 at http://www.southasiaanalysis.org/%5Cpapers16%5Cpaper1570.html
28. Anand Kumar, "Extremist, but not at the fringe," *The Indian Express*, New Delhi, September 27, 2003, Jamaat Amir Matiur Rahman acknowledged at a press conference in Dhaka on August 5, 2003 that his party wanted to establish Islamic rule without using violence.
29. "Militants strike again on courts," *The Daily Star*, 04 October 2005, at http://www.thedailystar.net/2005/10/04/d5100401011.htm
30. JMB suicide bomber kills 2 judges: Wounded assassin held with bomb strapped to his thigh; leaflets seek Islamic judicial system, *The Daily Star*, 15 November 2005at http://www.thedailystar.net/2005/11/15/d5111501011.htm

31. Md. Firoz Alam, Attacks on NGOs : Stain on image, *The Daily Star*, 5 March 2005 at http://www.thedailystar.net/2005/03/05/d50305020428.htm
32. Anand Kumar, Bangladesh-Islamists Attack NGOs as Part of Jihad, *South Asia Analysis Group*, Paper no. 1295, 21 March 2005, at http://southasiaanalysis.org/%5Cpapers13%5Cpaper1295.html
33. Two more JMJB men held, *The Daily Star,* 7 February 2005 at http://www.thedailystar.net/2005/02/07/d50207011311.htm
34. Bruce Vaughn, "Islamist Extremism in Bangladesh," *CRS Report for Congress*, January 31, 2007, p.1 at http://www.fas.org/sgp/crs/row/RS22591.pdf
35. Anand Kumar, "Dilemma for Donors in Bangladesh," *South Asia Analysis Group*, Paper no. 1313, 31 March 2005 at http://www.southasiaanalysis.org/papers14/paper1313.html
36. Delawar Hussain, "Bangladeshis in East London: From Secular Politics to Islam," Open Democracy at http://www.opendemocracy.net/democracy-protest/bangladeshi_3715.jsp
37. "More Britons travelling to Bangladesh to train in terror" Richard Norton-Taylor, *The Guardian,* Monday July 9 2007 at http://www.guardian.co.uk/uk/2007/jul/09/terrorism.bangladesh
38. This was learnt after a visit to the National Democratic Institute of Bangladesh. It is part of the USAID.
39. Based on interview with a former military advisor to the Bangladesh government.

5

Influence of Bangladesh on Northeast Insurgency

Northeast India has been gripped by insurgency from 1956 because of ethnic separatism. Besides this region has all other enabling conditions which a terrorist or insurgent outfit might need for conducting their activities. Ninety eight percent of Northeast is contiguous with the international border which allows terrorists to have sanctuaries in Bhutan, Myanmar, Bangladesh and even China where they can be trained and procure arms and ammunition from there. The ineffective administration in northern Myanmar, support of the intelligence agencies of Pakistan and Bangladesh and a regular flow of funds from narcotics smuggling in the Golden Triangle make their operations even easier. This environment was exploited by previous Bangladeshi governments to keep the region in turmoil. In this, they often acted in concert with Pakistan and its intelligence agency ISI.

Bangladesh is important in the context of Northeast insurgency because almost all insurgent groups of the region had their camps in that country. Barring the Awami League government of the country, other civilian and military governments of the country have been supportive of the insurgent groups. There is an interesting similarity between their approach and that of Pakistan. This has allowed Pakistani intelligence agency ISI to operate from Bangladesh in collaboration with the DGFI. They have been involved in the funding, training and arming of these rebel groups because they want to achieve their objectives through them. Islamic parties regularly talk of a Greater Bangladesh while the ISI support separatist elements in the Northeast so as to have an autonomous state in the region.

In recent times many of these Northeastern insurgent groups have become weaker but the external forces inimical to India are trying to keep the pot boiling in Northeast. They are trying to make many of these groups work in concert. ISI and the DGFI also created some Muslim extremist organisations in northeast and used the existing ones for their purposes. Some of them are present in Assam while few of them are also active in Manipur.

The Indian Insurgent Groups (IIGs) are now increasingly under external influence because declining support for ULFA has influenced its objectives. As of now the Indian insurgents appear to have become a tactical tool in the hands of ISI to fulfil its long-term objectives. In some cases, only the façade of the earlier outfit remains is left, whereas their objectives have completely changed. These outfits also seem to be losing their autonomy of action and are acting more at the behest of outside powers.

Bangladesh: A Safe Haven for Northeast Insurgents

Bangladesh has been a safe haven for Northeastern insurgents since its East Pakistan days. Though officially the Bangladesh government till 2008 asserted that it has "never allowed or assisted insurgent groups of any country for acts against that country and this policy was being pursued by the Government consistently and rigorously",[1] the actual policy of Bangladesh government was completely different. The top leaders and rank and file of many terrorist outfits have been staying in Bangladesh. This became very clear after action was taken against them during the second term of the Sheikh Hasina in January 2009.

Pro-Insurgent Record of the BNP and Military Governments

Indian insurgents have received major support from the military and the BNP led regimes. Under the BNP led governments this support has been direct. However, when Awami League is in power insurgents get support from only a section of the Bangladeshi security establishment. As a result, almost all Northeastern groups engaged in insurgency in northeast have camps in Bangladesh. Begum Khaleda Zia in her last stint as leader of the opposition had hailed these insurgents as "brave freedom fighters" carrying out a "heroic battle against an oppressive regime".[2]

When Sheikh Hasina came to power for the first time, she disbanded most of the "overground" training camps of these insurgents but could do nothing to those "underground" which continued with the assistance of various government intelligence agencies. It was during the Awami League's government that the ULFA leader Anup Chetia was arrested, convicted and jailed, while there were up to four attempts on the life of Paresh Barua the leader of the group's armed wing.

This forced Paresh Barua to leave Dhaka for Karachi. He returned to Bangladesh again after the victory of BNP in the elections. Though Karachi was safe, it was too far off and it was difficult to run a rebellion in Assam from there. Besides, Barua also owns a number of businesses in Bangladesh that funded his once-powerful group.

The insurgency in Manipur too has received support from Bangladesh. The United National Liberation Front (UNLF) was formed on 24 November 1964, under the leadership of Areambam Samarendra Singh for establishing an independent socialist Manipur. This outfit shared a close 'political relationship' with the then East Pakistani regime, and in 1969 its cadres underwent military training in that country. The group is also said to have backed the Pakistani army during the Bangladesh liberation war in 1971. In December 1968, a breakaway group of the UNLF, led by Oinam Sudhir Kumar, formed the Revolutionary Government of Manipur (RGM) with headquarters in Sylhet and was backed by Pakistan. However, the Meitei secessionist movement received a serious jolt when most of its leaders were arrested during the Bangladesh liberation war in 1971. Subsequently, the UNLF also became close to China and a team headed by N. Bisheswar Singh went to Lhasa in 1975 to seek Beijing's assistance. The UNLF is also close to the NSCN-K and has training camps in Myanmar and Bangladesh. In recent years insurgency has got intensified in Manipur and situation has become further complicated with rise of Islamist groups like PULF.

Similarly, in Tripura, both the major outlawed rebel groups—National Liberation Front of Tripura (NLFT) and the All Tripura Tiger Force (ATTF) fighting for independent tribal homelands have operated from bases in adjoining Bangladesh. Tripura shares a 856-kilometre-long border with Bangladesh with large part of the boundary unfenced and only concrete pillars separating the two countries. But Dhaka denies the presence of Indian rebel bases in their territory. The role of Bangladesh has been an important factor for the continuation of insurgency in Tripura.

Arms Smuggling

Bangladesh has also been supporting insurgency in the Northeast by freely allowing the smuggling of arms from its territory. There were several arms seizures in the year 2003. Substantial caches of arms have been recovered from Chittagong and its three hill districts; Bogra in north western Bangladesh; and even from the capital, Dhaka. Cox Bazar in Bangladesh has emerged as a major port for supply of illegal arms and ammunition to Northeast insurgents.[3]

The Bangladesh police and coastguard made the largest arms seizure in the history of the country, when they raided the government-controlled Chittagong Urea Fertiliser Limited (CUFL) jetty on 2 April 2004.[4] This seizure was made while the smugglers were unloading the weapons with the help of the local police.

The Awami League after coming to power has restarted investigations in the Chittagong arms seizure.[5] It has unmasked the government officials and agencies involved in arms trafficking. The investigation has now also conclusively proved that the arms were meant for Northeast insurgents.[6] The arrested smugglers have revealed that senior political leaders along with civil and military intelligence chiefs of then Khaleda Zia government were involved in the botched arms shipment.[7] The Sheikh Hasina government prosecuted two former Bangladesh army generals, Major General Rezakul Haider Chowdhury and Brigadier General Abdur Rahim, who headed the National Security Intelligence (NSI).[8] They were prosecuted for facilitating the landing of Chinese arms and for trying to smuggle these arms into India. It is also reported that Paresh Barua himself supervised the unloading of arms.[9]

Fratricidal Killings Among Insurgent Outfits in Dhaka

The insurgent groups using Bangladesh territory for terror operations against India have often indulged in fratricidal killings. This has further confirmed the presence of these groups in that country. Besides, the Bangladesh security agencies have often acted against these groups to keep the internal security situation under control. Dhaka has however denied all such incidents just to prove that insurgents are not using its territory.

In November 2009, the Sheikh Hasina government in Bangladesh took a significant step towards improving bilateral relations with India when it detained two top leaders of the ULFA—'foreign secretary' Sashadhar Choudhury and 'finance secretary' Chitraban Hazarika and handed them over to India.[10] Subsequently, they have also handed over ULFA chairman Arabinda Rajkhowa, his bodyguard Raja Bora and the Deupty Commander-in-Chief of ULFA Raju Barua. This signified a change in the attitude of Bangladesh towards Indian insurgent groups.

Bangladesh has also arrested and handed over Ranjan Daimary alias D.R. Nabla, the founder of the National Democratic Front of Bodoland. He is also the man behind Assam's most terrifying serial blasts.[11] But there are other top insurgent leaders who are still residing in Bangladesh. They are

Biswamohan Deb Barma of the NLFT and Ranjit Deb Barma of the ATTF. Both these outfits also have camps in Bangladesh.[12] Paresh Barua has already managed to escape on a 'Bangladeshi passport.' However, the current cooperation of Bangladesh would pacify New Delhi to some extent.

Islamist Groups in Northeast

The forces inimical to India are also trying to use Islamist groups of the Northeast to create disturbances in the region. They have also been working in tandem with Indian insurgent groups. There is a significant Muslim presence in Northeast India for centuries. Radical groups have emerged from the migrant Bangladeshi population and from among the Manipuri Muslims. The failure of people of Bangladesh origin to mix with the local Assamese people socially or culturally has created a lasting divide between them. This has been deepened by the changing demographic profile. The demolition of Babri Masjid and Maitei-Pangal riots of 1993 also had their impact.

A large number of Islamist groups exist in the Northeast—with an estimated 14 to 20 in Assam, and about five in Manipur. But only a few of them have any significant following. Some Islamic fundamentalist outfits which have tried to establish a foothold in Assam are: Harkat-ul-Jihad-al Islami Bangladesh (HuJI-B), Harkat-ul-Mujahideen (HuM), Islamic Liberation Army of Assam, Islamic Sevak Sangha, Muslim United Liberation Front of Assam (MULFA), Muslim United Liberation Tigers of Assam (MULTA), United Reformation Protest of Assam, Islamic United Revolution Protect of India (IURPI), People's United Liberation Front (PULF) and the Muslim Volunteer Force. A large population of Bangladeshi immigrants, especially in border areas, makes it easier for these organisations to operate. In Manipur the most important Islamist outfit is PULF which is a jihadi outfit and is believed to have links with Pakistan's ISI and other jihadi outfits in the region.[13] HuJI sleeper cells are also suspected to be operating in Nagaland.[14]

According to senior police officials in Assam, jihadi and other foreign elements have been active in Assam since 1994, when youths from the state were sent to the neighbouring country for training in terror camps. Pakistan's ISI is supporting the jihadis to destabilise India. When Bangladeshi Muslim militants were unable to go to Afghanistan following the installation of a civil government there, they turned their attention to the Indian Northeast. The recruitment of jihadis in the state is an ongoing process."[15] Between 2001 to 2006, in Assam at least 198 jihadis were arrested and another 58 surrendered. In the latter half of 2006 two Jama'atul Mujaheedin Bangladesh cadres—Badrul Alam in West Bengal and Habibur Rahman at Rangiya in Assam were arrested.

The propaganda by both Bangladeshi as well as Indian extremists has been partly responsible for the growing Islamic extremism in the Northeast. The two most important Indian groups engaged in propaganda are Students Islamic Movement of India (SIMI) and the Tabligi Jamaat. SIMI is suspected of having links with the Islami Chhatra Shibir of Bangladesh and the Jamaat-e-Islami. Tabligi Jamaat also has a significant presence in Bangladesh.

Islamist groups of Bangladesh have also been active in West Bengal.[16] They have not only been recruiting jihadis from India but also sending their fundamentalist leaders to campaign in the border states of India.

Among the Bangladeshi groups engaged in terrorist activities the HuJI poses the greatest threat. The HuJI is believed to be of Pakistani origin, set up in Bangladesh in April 1992 by Pakistani intelligence to drum up a violent anti-India Islamic militant movement.[17] HuJI is believed to be part of a loose terror network that includes the Lashkar-e-Taiba.[18] According to West Bengal police, there is coordination and manpower exchange between at least 10 Islamic militant groups, including the HuJI and the LeT, all along the eastern border of the country, and in the innumerable sleeper cells in the suburban parts of the state. They have not indulged in violence in the state because that would make them lose an important base.[19] It is suspected that the LeT has set up a new wing called the Tanzeem-e-Mohammedi to create unrest in the Northeastern states and the districts of West Bengal bordering Bangladesh.[20]

The coming together of HuJI-B and terrorist outfits operating out of Pakistan like LeT is disconcerting. This became clear when the HuJI's operation commander Abdul Hannan after being arrested in October 2005 admitted that he had passed out of the Gouhardanga madrassa in Pakistan. This was further authenticated by the arrest of his brother Matiur Rehman, accused of conspiring to kill Bangladesh leader Sheikh Hasina, whose personal diary revealed that he was in constant touch with Pakistan's diplomatic mission in Dhaka.[21]

Arrests taking place in Bangladesh since May 2009 have now completely proven this link. The Bangladesh police arrested Moulana Mohammad Mansur Ali, an Indian national linked with the Pakistan-based LeT from a madrassa in Dakkhin Khan area of Dhaka on 20 July 2009.[22] He was also an organiser of Asif Reza Commando Force, the terrorist outfit responsible for the attack on American Centre in Kolkata on 22 January 2002. This arrest was made on the basis of information gleaned from Mufti Obaidullah, another Indian and LeT operative captured in Dhaka few days ago in 2009.[23] Police also had got information about these operatives from Daud Merchant and Zahid Sheikh two henchmen of the notorious gangster and terrorist Dawood Ibrahim who were arrested on 27 May 2009.[24] These arrests also indicated that LeT was funding some of the HuJI activities in Bangladesh.[25]

When the JMB was on the rise in Bangladesh, it sent its cadres to the Northeast. It also had operational control over jihadis in the Northeast.[26] The JMB had planned to kill Assam chief minister Tarun Gogoi because of his firm stand to prevent upsurge of Islamic militancy in Assam and for this purpose the outfit even formed suicide squads.[27] At one point the JMB even out did the ISI and HuJI and started controlling Islamic militant outfits in Bangladesh and reaching out to groups across the northeast.[28]

The Indian home ministry in a report indicated that terror elements from Bangladesh used Karimganj and Dhubri districts as "corridors" to sneak into India. According to official records security forces arrested 538 suspected jihadi elements in the run-up to the 2009 Lok Sabha elections. Of them, 312 were arrested in Karimganj and 226 in Dhubri. The report also confirmed the existence of a number of sleeper cells in the state.[29]

Replying to a question in Assam state assembly, the forest minister, Rockybul Hussain stated that as many as eight militant groups including two fundamentalist outfits were active in Assam, and between May, 2001 and 30 June 2009, 8,783 militants were arrested and 1,417 were killed by the security forces. He also informed that among the fundamentalist forces, the Muslim United Liberation Tigers of Assam (MULTA) has around 140 members, while, the Harkat-ul-Muzahideen (HuM) has around 42 members. Giving an account of the estimated strength of the militant groups active in the State, Hussain said that the ULFA has around 1100 members; the KLNLF, 210 members; the KRA about 35; HPC (D) has around 40; the AANLA about 45 and the DHD (J) around 230. Hussain informed the House that so far 58 ISI operatives, HuJI and HuM members have been arrested, of whom seven were ISI operatives, four were members of the HuJI and the rest were members of the HUM. Seven fundamentalist elements are still in different jails in the state.[30] The minister also revealed that of the militant groups active in Assam, the top leaders of the ULFA and NDFB are hiding in various places in Bangladesh.

Weakening Support Base of Northeast Insurgents

Except for Manipur, insurgency in the whole of the Northeast is on the decline. Insurgent groups like ULFA, NLFT, ATTF, NDFB etc have been considerably weakened. After 9/11 international opinion decisively turned against terrorism. This has also resulted in the ULFA being branded a terrorist organisation by the US. The ULFA was also weakened when Bhutan launched its operation against the IIGs in December 2003.

Along with the international situation the domestic situation also turned against terrorists and there have been desertions from their rank because of disillusionment. While the cadres were facing hardships in jungles, the leaders were enjoying opulent lifestyles in Bangladesh. Organisations have also faced stress on the grounds of ideology. The discontent even led to a split in ULFA. The organisation has now been divided into pro-talk and anti-talk factions. Even the most deadly 28 battalion of ULFA declared ceasefire and opted for talks. The continuing operations by the Indian security forces also put pressure on insurgent outfits.

The ULFA has tried to replenish its cadre base by reaching out to new recruits from among the Adivasis or tea tribes. It also tried to engage in terror activities in concert with other insurgent outfits. But these tactics were not very helpful.

ULFA's International Linkages

ULFA suffered major reverses in the Bhutanese operation. Even the counter-insurgency operations of Indian security forces in Northeast have been quite successful. Despite these ULFA has not sought a ceasefire or peace talks because it is still able to run its operations from its camps in Bangladesh and Myanmar. Though its Commander-in-chief Paresh Barua has been forced to leave Dhaka he still has good contacts in Bangladesh. Till very recently most of ULFA's top leadership was based in Bangladesh. The business interests of ULFA in Bangladesh are another reason why this outfit is reluctant to come to the negotiation table.

Bangladesh as an Operational Zone for ISI

The relations between Bangladesh and Pakistan were strained in the aftermath of the liberation war. Subsequently however they improved dramatically as both countries wanted to balance India in the subcontinent. Pakistan recognised Bangladesh in 1974 and established diplomatic relations two years later. On the other hand, India's obsession with Pakistan made it ignore Bangladesh. Some also suspect that during his visit to Bangladesh in 2003 the Pakistan president Pervez Musharraf tried to forge covert military ties with Dhaka and obtain clearance for the ISI to operate from Bangladeshi territory.[31]

The ISI has tried to spread its tentacles in the Northeast through the IIGs. For ISI, Bangladesh has become an operational zone for bleeding India and ensuring a large deployment of its army in the east away from Kashmir and the Pakistan border. Besides, it is also interested in carving an independent state out of India to avenge the separation of Bangladesh. ISI has been involved in funding, training and arming these rebel groups in order to keep India tied down.

Pressure in Myanmar exerted by its security forces led groups like the ULFA to establish contacts with the ISI and Afghan Mujahideen in Pakistan.[32] In March 1994 the Assam Assembly was informed that some 200 ULFA militants have reportedly received training with the help of Pakistan's ISI, many of them in Afghanistan, over the previous two years.[33] This relationship only deepened in subsequent years.

To facilitate its work, ISI has tried to take the help of fundamentalist elements within Bangladesh government, army, bureaucracy and intelligence. The ISI has been instrumental, either directly or through the Pakistan High Commission in Dhaka, in developing a nexus between IIGs, Islamic fundamentalists and criminal elements in Bangladesh. Besides assisting terrorists in the procurement of arms, ammunition and explosives, the ISI has been arranging meetings of terrorists of different hues to coordinate their activities.[34]

The game-plan of ISI has been known since at least 7 August 1999 when Assam police achieved a major breakthrough, and busted an ISI network in the state, arresting 31 people, including two ISI officers and 27 militants belonging to different Islamic militant outfits. Arrested operatives revealed the objectives of the ISI in the Northeastern region, which were:

- To raise a large group of Muslim youth fighters from Assam
- To use ULFA etc to create large-scale disturbances in the entire region.
- To launch a two-pronged economic war by taking money collected by the underground elements to Pakistan and by inundating the area with fake and counterfeit currency notes.
- To foment communal trouble in Assam
- To introduce the smuggling of narcotics and link it with terrorism

The arrests of ISI operatives also led to the uncovering of the activities of Islamists in the districts of Barpeta, Goalpara, Dhubri and Nalbari in Assam.[35] The arrests in Guwahati were the first arrests of any 'ISI operatives' in the country. Two of these were Pakistani nationals—Mohammad Fasiullah Hussaini alias Hamid Mahmood alias Khalid Mehmood of Hyderabad (Sind) and Mohammad Javed Waqar alias Mohammad Mustafa Abdul Rahman Danish of Karachi. Both of them were alleged to be top activists of the Pakistan-based HuM. However, nine years after they were arrested, four persons, including Fasiullah Hussaini and Mohammad Javed Waqar, were released by a sessions court in Guwahati on 11 June due to lack of 'solid evidence.' Along with these two Pakistanis nationals a Bangladeshi national Bilal Miyan, arrested from West Bengal, was also released. All of them were acquitted of the charges of waging war against India, criminal conspiracy and sedition. Their acquittal triggered a hue and cry in the state with All Assam Students Union accusing the Congress-led government in the state of making a weak case against the 'ISI operatives'.[36]

A report presented in the Assam State Assembly on 6 April 2000 stated that the Assam police had in its possession plenty of evidence to show that the top ULFA leadership was in close touch with certain officials of the Pakistani High Commission in Dhaka. The ULFA leaders had also been travelling to Pakistan regularly and the Pakistani officials in Dhaka arranged for their passports in various Muslim names.[37]

In April 2002 ISI took a major initiative to unite several Islamic rebel organisations in Assam and across the North-East, with major insurgent groups of the region receiving instructions to impart training to these rebels. They also attempted to rope in several Manipur-based Islamic outfits like the Peoples United Liberation Front and the Islamic Liberation Army. Through this effort the ISI wanted to step up disruptive activities. The Pakistan High Commission in Dhaka organised a meeting in this regard. This meeting was attended by three top leaders of the ULFA and the ISI in charge for North-Eastern affairs. The meeting held in January 2002 was to finalise the arms training for the Islamic rebels where the ULFA gave in to the ISI demand.

On 9-10 May 2002, 63 representatives of nine Islamic groups including Rohingya forces, the Islamic Oikya Jote and the ULFA met in Ukhia to form the Bangladesh Islamic Manch, a united council under HuJI leadership. The Manch has big plans of creating an Islamic country beyond the territorial limits of Bangladesh that will include Muslim areas of Assam, north Bengal and Myanmar's Arakan province.[38]

Increasing External Influence over Insurgents

In recent times, ISI has further intensified its focus on the Indian Northeast. In January 2008 the Assam police arrested S.M. Alam a Bangladeshi national. He was a top-ranking member of the Bangladesh Islamic Chhatra Shibir, and was appointed the "Northeast in-charge" by the ISI. He was a conduit between the ISI and the region's outfits with the help of ULFA's help. Alam selected 40 youths from 24 outfits across the region for training in Pakistan-occupied Kashmir.[39] This shows that a large number of insurgent groups in Northeast are now controlled by Islamic militants.[40] The ISI had directed ULFA to buy arms for smaller insurgent groups from the profits accruing from its businesses in Bangladesh. The smaller outfits have always been supported by the bigger militant groups in the region, but external involvement injected a new element into militancy in the Northeast[41] which indicated a seamless link between the ISI, Jamaat, Bangladesh Islamists and IIGs.

The external influence is clear in the case of ULFA. The ULFA claims to be a "revolutionary political organisation" engaged in a "liberation struggle" against India for a sovereign, independent Assam. The ULFA initially refrained from attacking civilian targets and vital installations in Assam. But over the years, the group has come to be increasingly influenced by the ISI and DGFI. It is also believed that Paresh Barua is no longer a free man and acts at the behest of the ISI.

The degeneration of ULFA was manifested in the Dhemaji blasts, in which several school children were killed.[42] ULFA has now also been killing Hindi speaking people. But when even that failed to have desired impact, it started planting bombs in crowded places in which innocent people—even those of Assamese origin were killed making it amply clear that ULFA was not fighting for the rights and identity of the Assamese people.

It is common knowledge that Paresh Barua and his family members have been living in a posh locality of Dhaka for long and have adopted the Islamic way of life.[43] But recent intelligence reports claim that Barua has converted to Islam along with his family members. What is more, he has now got married for the second time to a Bangladeshi woman.[44] This development is significant as ULFA now has been reduced to one man show. If the ISI and DGFI have complete control over Paresh Barua then Barua in his turn exercises complete control over ULFA. Though the outfit has several other prominent leaders like Arvinda Rajkhowa, Sashdhar Chowdhury and Raju Barua, but they matter little in the organisation. Paresh Barua controls both the financial and arms channels of the outfit.[45] This also enables him to take all the major policy decision. Now it can well be assumed what kind of decisions he would take under the influence of ISI and DGFI.

In the year 2008, the ULFA ranks rose in revolt against the proximity of its top leaders with Bangladeshi groups, which resulted in the A and C company of ULFA's 28 battalion declaring a unilateral cease fire. This potent wing of the outfit decided to join the national mainstream with top leaders including Mrinal Hazarika, Joon Bhuyan and Jiten Dutta, leading the cadres.[46] These cadres also tried to persuade Paresh Barua who refused to listen to them.

There also appears to be a disconnect between Paresh Barua and the rank and file. Most ULFA cadres have not even seen him. Even the photograph available with the security agencies is very old. In these circumstances, it is not surprising that the ideology has been turned on its head. The rank and file still believe that they are fighting for the original cause for which ULFA was created. But in reality the outfit is now a completely different animal.

ULFA and other insurgents have now completely lost their autonomy. They are acting at the behest of ISI, DGFI and Islamists. They are now completely terrorist outfits devoid of any ideology. Though the ULFA is sticking to its demand for a sovereign Assam as a precondition for talks with the government of India, it has compromised on the issue with forces inimical to India. In ULFA's new scheme of things the sovereign Assam will exist within the overall Islamic republic in the Northeast.

The ULFA began in 1979 as a violent movement to drive away foreigners who were threatening Assam's language, culture and political voice. But that ULFA no longer exists. The ULFA in its present shape considers the same outsiders as its friends and people from other parts of India as its enemy.

Mrinal Hazarika, the "lieutenant" heading the ceasefire-bound companies of ULFA's 28th battalion, feels that ULFA has paid dearly for its alliance with the Islamists as they have lost credibility on the international forums. He said:

> The top ULFA leadership has close links with the ISI, Directorate General of Field Intelligence (the Bangladeshi intelligence agency) and some Islamic organisations. Without their support, it is not possible for anyone to have bases in Bangladesh. [47]

Despite the growing influence of Islamist groups over the ULFA an attempt has often been made to highlight the militant ethno-nationalist nature of the outfit and its Hindu origin. Some also deemed it as being similar to the Liberation Tigers of Tamil Eelam in Sri Lanka. It was pointed out that any coordination between the ULFA and religiously motivated non-state actors in Bangladesh and Pakistan would be of an operational nature based on temporarily dovetailing of interests rather than any ideological commonality.[48] A section in Assam still believes this. Probably this is the reason why ULFA still manages to get some recruits.

Notes

1. "Reports on arrest of Indian militants in Dhaka false: home ministry," *The Daily Star*, 4 January 2004 at http://www.thedailystar.net/2004/01/04/d40104011616.htm
2. Anand Kumar, "External Influences on the Northeast Insurgency,"*AGNI*(New Delhi) Voume XII, Number II, January-March 2010, p. 40 at http://fsss.in/agni-volume/2nd/external-influences-on-the-northeast-insurgency.pdf
3. Saswati Chanda and Alok Kumar Gupta, "Pakistan-Bangladesh Nexus in Abetting Insurgency in India's Northeast," in Dipankar Sengupta and Sudhir Kumar Singh edited *"Insurgency in North-East India: The Role of Bangladesh,"* Authors Press, New Delhi, 2004, p. 279.
4. "Delhi worried over Bangla arms haul" Rediff.com, 12 April 2004, at http://www.rediff.com/news/2004/apr/12bang.htm
5. "Pursuing the biggest arms haul case," *The Daily Star* (Dhaka), 6 March 2009 at http://www.thedailystar.net/newDesign/news-details.php?nid=78550
6. "Arms found in Bangladesh meant for Indian insurgent group," IANS, June 9th, 2009 at http://www.thaindian.com/newsportal/world-news/arms-found-in-bangladesh-meant-for-indian-insurgent-group_100202554.html
7. "Zia government behind botched ULFA arms shipment," *The Hindu,* 5 March 2009 at http://www.thehindu.com/holnus/001200903051011.htm
8. Dhaka to prosecute 2 former spy chiefs smuggling arms for Indian rebels, IANS, 18 May, 2009 at http://www.thaindian.com/newsportal/world-news/dhaka-to-prosecute-2-former-spy-chiefs-smuggling-arms-for-indian-rebels_100194036.html also see, "Ctg Arms Haul: Top intelligence men partners in crime," *The Daily Star* (Dhaka) 9 March 2009, at http://www.thedailystar.net/story.php?nid=79054
9. "Indian rebel leaders were in Chittagong," *The Daily Star,* March 8, 2009, at http://www.thedailystar.net/newDesign/news-details.php?nid=78893
10. Border Security Force arrest two ULFA leaders along India-Bangladesh border, *The Times of India,* 7 November 2009 at http://timesofindia.indiatimes.com/india/Border-Security-Force-arrest-two-ULFA-leaders-along-India-Bangladesh-border/articleshow/5204738.cms, also see "Assam unveils Ulfa leaders caught in Bangladesh," *The Telegraph* (Kolkata), November 8 , 2009, at http://www.telegraphindia.com/1091108/jsp/nation/story_11714009.jsp#
11. Daimary arrest triggers hope of parleys, *The Telegraph*, 3 May 2010 at http://www.telegraphindia.com/1100503/jsp/frontpage/story_12404969.jsp , also see "Daimary arrest shot in the arm for Indian diplomacy," *The Assam Tribune*, 4 May 2010 at http://www.assamtribune.com/scripts/detailsnew.asp?id=may0410/at06
12. 'Ultras still have camps in Bangladesh', *The Assam Tribune*, 6 January 2011 at http://www.assamtribune.com/scripts/detailsnew.asp?id=jan0611/oth06
13. PULF-ISI nexus exposed again, terrorists caught, *Times Now*, 19 Jul 2009 at http://www.timesnow.tv/PULF-ISI-nexus-exposed-again-terrorists-caught/articleshow/4322592.cms, also see "7 PULF members nabbed in Tripura," *E-Pao*, 18 July 2009 at http://www.e-pao.net/GP.asp?src=21..190709.jul09
14. 'Muslim NSCN (I-M) operatives in touch with HuJI', *The Indian Express*, 17 August 2009 at http://www.indianexpress.com/news/muslim-nscn-im-operatives-in-touch-with-huji/503053/0
15. "Jihadis infiltrating North-east: Official," PTI, November 02, 2006, http://www.rediff.com///news/2006/nov/02assam.htm
16. Ramananda Sengupta, "Why India is concerned about Bangladesh," December 22, 2005, http://news.rediff.com/news/2005/dec/22bspec.htm

17. Ramtanu Maitra, "Saudis stoke South Asian fears," *Asia Times* online, 23 November 2004 http://www.atimes.com/atimes/South_Asia/FK23Df02.html
18. Jyoti Thottam / Panidhar, "A Great Divide," *Time*, 5 February 2009, http://www.time.com/time/printout/0,8816,1877200,00.html
19. Haroon Habib, Suhrid Sankar Chattopadhyay, "Challenges in the east," *Frontline*, Vol. 23, Iss 01, URL: http://www.flonnet.com/fl2301/stories/20060127006201100.htm
20. Ravik Bhattacharya, "Lashkar has new face in east—Tanzeem-e-Mohammedi," *The Indian Express*, 9 March, 2009 at http://www.expressindia.com/story_print.php?storyId= 432613
21. "HuJI, LeT joining hands rattles security agencies," *The Times of India*, 1 November 2008, http://timesofindia.indiatimes.com/rssarticleshow/msid-3660696,prtpage-1.cms
22. "Top LeT militant held in Dhaka" *The Indian Express*, 22 July 2009 at http://www.indianexpress.com/story-print/492460/ , also see, "Another Lashkar man captured: The Indian national linked to attack on American Centre in Kolkata" *The Daily Star*, 22 July 2009 at http://www.thedailystar.net/newDesign/news-details.php?nid=98023
23. Haroon Habib, "Wanted militant arrested in Bangladesh," *The Hindu*, 19 July 2009 at http://www.hindu.com/thehindu/thscrip/print.pl?file=2009071954680900.htm&date=2009/07/19/&prd=th& also see, "Nabbed terrorist talked daily with Pak boss on phone: Bangladesh," *The Hindustan Times*, 19 July 2009 at http://www.hindustantimes.com/world-news/Bangladesh/Nabbed-Indian-militant-talked-daily-with-boss-in-Pakistan-Dhaka/Article1-433933.aspx
24. "Another Lashkar man captured: The Indian national linked to attack on American Centre in Kolkata," *The Daily Star*, July 22, 2009, at http://www.thedailystar.net/newDesign/news-details.php?nid=98023
25. "Laskar-e-Taiyeba funds HuJI activities," *The Daily Star*, 19 July 2009 at http://www.thedailystar.net/newDesign/latest_news.php?nid=18166
26. "Jihadis infiltrating North-east: Official," PTI, November 02, 2006, http://www.rediff.com///news/2006/nov/02assam.htm
27. K Anurag, Assam CM threatened by fundamentalists, September 12, 2006 at http://www.rediff.com/news/2006/sep/12assam.htm
28. Samudra Gupta Kashyap, "Bangla militants controlling N-E groups, says Assam DGP," *The Indian Express*, Nov 03, 2006 at http://www.indianexpress.com/story_print.php?storyid=15916
29. "Security forces step up operations against jihadis," *Times of India*, April 28, 2009, at http://articles.timesofindia.indiatimes.com/2009-04-28/guwahati/28038572_1_bsf-personnel-jihadis-bangladeshi
30. "1,417 ultras killed since 2001," *Assam Tribune*, July 14, 2009 at http://www.assamtribune.com/scripts/details.asp?id=jul1409/at05
31. Harsh V. Pant, "India and Bangladesh: Will the Twain Ever Meet?," *Asian Survey*, Vol. 47, No. 2 (March/April 2007), pp. 234-235
32. B.G. Verghese, p58
33. B.G. Verghese, pp59-60
34. Sultan Shahin, "India frets over Pakistan-Bangladesh nexus," *Asia Times* online, March 6, 2004 at http://www.atimes.com/atimes/South_Asia/FC06Df02.html
35. K Anurag, "Northeast India gears up against terror attacks," *Rediff News*, July 16, 2006 at http://www.rediff.com///news/2006/jul/16terror.htm
36. "Assam vulnerable to Islamic terror groups," *Rediff News*, November 01, 2008, http://world.rediff.com/news/article/www/news/2008/nov/01assam.htm
37. Jaideep Saikia, "The ISI Reaches East: Anatomy of a Conspiracy," *Studies in Conflict & Terrrorism*,"Routledge, Volume 25, Issue 3 May 2002, pp. 191-192.

38. Alex Perry, "Deadly Cargo," *Time,* 14 October, 2002 at http://www.time.com/time/magazine/article/0,9171,364423-2,00.html
39. Nishit Dholabhai, "ISI funds N-E rebels, says agent," *The Telegraph*, January 18, 2008, http://www.telegraphindia.com/1080118/jsp/northeast/story_8796908.jsp#
40. Nava Thakuria, "ISI Spreads a Net in Northeast India," *The Seoul Times,* http://theseoultimes.com/ST/?url=/ST/db/read.php?idx=6239
41. Nishit Dholabhai, "ISI funds N-E rebels, says agent," *The Telegraph,* January 18, 2008, http://www.telegraphindia.com/1080118/jsp/northeast/story_8796908.jsp#
42. "Five years later, Paresh sorry for Dhemaji," *The Telegraph*, 14 December 2009 at http://www.telegraphindia.com/1091214/jsp/northeast/story_11859330.jsp
43. Jaideep Saikia, *Terror Sans Frontiers: Islamist Militancy in North East India*, Vision Books, New Delhi, 2004, p. 85. Interrogation report of arrested ULFA cadre John Barua clearly shows this.
44. Based on interview of several senior intelligence officers and journalists.
45. Ibid.
46. Sanjoy Ray, "2008 saw emergence of Islamic militancy in State," *Assam Tribune*, December 26, 2008 http://www.assamtribune.com/scripts/details.asp?id=dec2608/at08
47. Nishit Dholabhai, "Ulfa peaceniks spill beans: Pro-talks group confirms outfit's links with ISI & Bangla," *The Telegraph*, 7 February 2009.
48. Derek Henry Flood, "Motivations and Methods of India's United Liberation Front of Asom (ULFA)," *Terrorism Monitor,* The Jamestown Foundation, Vol. 7, Issue 9, 10 April 2009 at http://www.jamestown.org/programs/gta/single/?tx_ttnews%5Btt_news%5D=34840&tx_ttnews%5BbackPid%5D=412&no_cache=1

6

Financing of Terror Groups

Terrorism is generally guided by an ideology but terror cannot make much headway without funds. Two types of terror activities have been taking place from Bangladesh. In one case, terror activities have been carried out by Islamic groups within Bangladesh with the objective of creating an Islamic state. However, at least one Islamist group HuJI has also been active against India. The other kind of terror activity is undertaken by Indian insurgent groups who use Bangladesh for running insurgency in Northeast India. The funding of both these groups comes from different sources.

There are two dimensions to the term 'terrorist financing.' It may refer to the ongoing fundraising efforts by which a terrorist organisation supports its overall operation, arms acquisition, political activity if needed, propaganda output and basic training of recruits. The second dimension is funding requirement for a specific terrorist operation. Funds are needed, for example, for the terrorist cell's food and accommodation, transport, safe houses, forged identity papers, and both legal and illegal bomb components. This money is raised from various sources, some of which are clearly illegal, but some part of it could also be completely legitimate at the point of donation.[1]

It is now generally felt that governments have to take steps to check terror financing to curb terrorist activities. The groundwork for this was prepared by the adoption of the International Convention for Suppression of the Financing of Terrorism in December 1999 as per which countries were expected to formulate laws to cut off the funding to terrorist organisations. During the BNP led four-party government there was a sudden rise in terror incidents in Bangladesh but the government kept dragging its feet. In recent times, the Bangladeshi authorities have been amenable to Indian requests for action against terror groups but their actions have been largely confined to raids, arrests and intelligence gathering. The government has not been as successful in controlling the finances of terror groups as the country lacks the requisite infrastructure and the political resolve at the top does not get reflected at lower level where the Jamaat has strong support.

Financing of Islamist Groups

Islamist groups have thrived in Bangladesh because of the conducive domestic and international environment and political patronage that they have received during the BNP led regimes and military governments before 1990. But these groups can't function unless they have significant funding. It has sometime been pointed out that terror groups in Bangladesh do not require much money because they use less sophisticated methods of terror strike. While it is true that a particular terror act may not require much money but funding is needed for maintenance of terror organisation and their continuous activity. This funding is necessary to keep their political activity going, recruit cadres and indoctrinate new sections of population. The cadres who often get killed in carrying out terror acts have to be compensated. Besides, a number of trans-national groups like LeT, JeM etc have also been active in Bangladesh who require considerable funds for their operation.

In Bangladesh, the previous four-party alliance government was not clear about its approach towards terrorism. Though it recognised terrorism as a scourge to be politically correct, confusion was created on its definition. It thwarted any serious action against the patrons and financiers of Islamist militancy though the country has acceded to 12 out of 13 UN conventions on terrorism.

It may not be possible to accurately estimate the volume of terrorist financing in Bangladesh but definitely an attempt can be made to identify the sources that finance terror in that country. During the four-party alliance rule the obfuscation of the issue of terrorism together with the lack of adequate state machinery and staff had rendered the existing laws ineffective. The present government of Sheikh Hasina however is trying to address some of these issues.

Main Beneficiary Groups and Institutions

The funding from various sources helped the Jamaat—which has been the political face of the extremist groups—and the AHAB. Both these organisations have maintained links with the Islamist militant groups like

JMJB, the JMB, Al Hikma, HuJI and many others. Money is used to expand their influence by recruiting youths and motivating and training them. The funds have also helped to set up many mosques and madrassas which have been instrumental in radicalising society at the district and village level.

Sources of Financing of Islamist Groups

There are various sources of funding for Islamist groups. A major part of the money comes from abroad but some part of it is also domestically generated.

Dubious Role of Some Islamic Charities/NGOs

Bangladesh has a huge NGO presence. These are of two kinds—Islamic and non-Islamic. Non-Islamic NGOs are generally engaged in development work, poverty alleviation, healthcare, gender equality and the majority of them receive foreign funding for their work. The non-Islamic NGOs have played a very important role in Bangladeshi society. In fact, these NGOs are credited with having stemmed the radicalisation of Bangladeshi society unlike Afghanistan and Pakistan.[2] These NGOs constitute the frontline in the war against terror.

It is, however, some Islamic NGOs that are the problem. The focus shifted towards these Islamic charities after the September 11 attacks. Since then the US has taken strong steps to halt the flow of funds to terrorist organisations under Executive Order 13224 and related elements of the USA Patriot Act.[3] Islamic charities became suspect as regulators worldwide feared that they would be a convenient conduit for funding violence. The financial scrutiny of these organisations is not as it should be and the trust-based nature of charitable work means that it is sometimes possible for an insider to fund terror from the financial flows meant for genuine purposes.[4]

Al-Haramain Islamic Foundation (AHIF)

The Al-Haramain Islamic Foundation (AHIF) was a large Riyadh-based Muslim charity which came under scanner after a string of deadly bombings linked to the al-Qaeda, rocked the Saudi kingdom in 2003. These attacks forced the Saudis to intensify the scrutiny of charities which led to the winding up of the AHIF, along with other Saudi charities. Their financial assets were transferred to the new Saudi National Commission for Relief and Charity Work Abroad subject to strict financial oversight. The step was taken to prevent charitable contributions from being siphoned off to finance terrorism.[5]

Saudi Arabia and the United States also jointly asked the United Nations to include the five branches of Al-Haramain among the blacklisted terrorist financiers. This was done with the objective of freezing their assets. One of the branches of Al-Haramain was located in Bangladesh.[6]

Al-Haramain had been active in Bangladesh since it opened an office in Cox's Bazaar in 1992 to help Rohingya refugees. In 1995 it opened an office in Dhaka and ran four orphanages in Uttara, Nilphamari and Gazipur and was maintaining 60 mosques across the country by June 2004. It spread its network to 38 districts and received a five-year grant of Tk 19.27 crore until 2001. The operation of Al-Haramain in Bangladesh continued unhindered months after it was banned by the US and Saudi Arabia.[7]

Alleged Terror Links

Seven Al-Haramain men were arrested by the Bangladesh police in their Uttara office in September 2002 for terror funding and trafficking in women and children in the garb of providing Islamic education. Although there were specific allegations against the members of the organisation, they were released after a few days by the police for lack of evidence. It is however believed that they were released under 'external pressure'.[8]

Proliferation of Islamic NGOs in Bangladesh

Islamic NGOs proliferated in Bangladesh after the 1991 cyclone that devastated Chittagong and other coastal areas of the country. Some 575 registered Islamic NGOs were active all over the country in 2005 which were funded by donations from Libya, Abu Dhabi, Saudi Arabia, Qatar, Kuwait, Iran and Egypt as well as India, Pakistan, the United Sates and the United Kingdom.[9] They conducted relief operations that included: providing shelter, supplying drinking water, setting up hospitals, running orphanages, sanitation, mother and child healthcare, apart from setting up religious educational institutions and preaching Islam. They also built several hundred mosques in villages with funds from the Middle East countries. There is no exact figure but according to one estimate the money sent to Bangladesh ranged between 4.0 billion taka to 5.0 billion taka (61.5 million to 76.9 million US dollars) per year in year 2005.[10] The Islamic NGOs in Bangladesh employ about 25,000 people. But what is concerning about these NGOs is that some among them, are front organisations for terror outfits, who are channelling funds from abroad to fuel terrorist activity in the country.

Islamic NGOs in Bangladesh are of two varieties—foreign and domestic.

Foreign NGOs

In 2005, there were 34 foreign funded major Islamic NGOs registered with the NGO Bureau of which around 15 were very active, getting over Tk 200 crore in donations every year. The amount received by them varied from Tk 5 crore to 70 crore each year, mainly from Saudi Arabia, Kuwait and the UAE. In some cases funds also come from the UK and the US. The donors sometimes form consortiums to fund these NGOs which makes it possible for countries even like Sudan to contribute though they may not be very rich. The NGOs include the Islamic Relief Organisation (IIRO), Al Markajul Islami, Ishra Islamic Foundation, Ishrahul Muslimin, Al Forkan Foundations and the Al Maghrib Eye Hospital.[11] These large Islamic NGOs are known as mother organisations, which sub-contract projects to small NGOs or give them funds.[12]

The functioning of the NGO bureau has been a concern given the numerous NGOs and charities in the country, and a total lack of financial transparency. The bureau has insufficient human resources to regulate the whole sector. This was highlighted by the Green Crescent case in March 2009. The bureau was further seen as being suspect as it came under the ministry of social welfare, held by the Jamaat from 2001-06. It is alleged that the 473 local and 25 foreign NGOs licenced during this period were not properly regulated. The funds coming to these organisations could have been misused given the Jamaat's links with some militant organistaions.

Local NGOs

There are several hundred local Islamic NGOs registered with the social welfare department. The number of such NGOs increased significantly after Jamaat secretary general Ali Ahsan Mohammad Mojaheed became social welfare minister.[13] As these NGOs work as affiliates of the foreign funded ones they do not account for their expenditure to the government.[14]

Islamic NGOs under Cloud after the Serial Blasts of August 2005

The serial bomb blasts that rocked Bangladesh on 17 August 2005 raised vital questions about the sources of finance of these militant outfits. This made the security agencies of Bangladesh sit up and take notice of the terror funding by Islamist NGOs and at least 10 were identified for channelling funds to various Islamist extremist outfits in the country. These were: the Revival of Islamic Heritage Society (RIHS), Rabita Al-Alam Al-Islami, Society of Social Reforms, Qatar Charitable Society, Al-Muntada Al-Islami, Islamic

Relief Agency, Al-Forkan Foundation, International Relief Organisation, Kuwait Joint Relief Committee and the Muslim Aid Bangladesh. The security agencies also investigated how these NGOs had been utilising the money prior to 17 August.

It was also found that more than 100 foreigners from various West Asian and African countries were working with these NGOs and were in the country illegally. They had come to Bangladesh on tourist visas and did not have work permits. All 10 NGOs are based in West Asia but have been active in Bangladesh for several years.

The RIHS banned in the US because of links with the Al Qaeda was at the top of the list of NGOs that were under the scanner. The security agencies of Bangladesh also advised the government to ban the RIHS. They also suspected the AHAB of routing the NGO's funds to the banned JMB.

The RIHS with assistance from AHAB built over 1000 mosques, 10 madrassas, four orphanages-cum-madrassas and a kidney dialysis centre at various places across the country. The mosques and madrassas were later found to be the hubs for the militant activities of the JMB.[15] The mosques and madrassas were allegedly used for the recruitment and motivation of fighters. Galib had also used the RIHS funds to finance the JMB's operations.

Galib confessed that he received around Tk 27 crore every year from the Middle East, especially from the RIHS of Kuwait. He spent the funds on the JMB, JMJB and al-Hiqma, which were all banned Islamist organisations. Galib was getting funds by cheque and cash and sometimes even by hundi. The investigators recovered a large number of computer documents, diaries, notes, books, booklets, leaflets and audio cassettes from Galib's house, and AHAB offices and madrassas in Rajshahi. Since Galib's arrest, the government has stopped disbursement of funds from RIHS.[16]

In some cases, funds from abroad apparently meant for religious work and construction of mosques and madrassas in Bangladesh were diverted for the jihadi cause. People like Galib used these funds to recruit and train jihadi fighters. Local NGOs that were working among orphans and the poor were denied funds meant for their work. The RIHS started funding madrassas in 1993 but stopped doing so in July 2001.[17] Seven madrassas located in Bogra, Rajshahi, Bagerhat and Satkhira districts were receiving funds until then, and the sudden stoppage of funds affected their capacity to provide food and housing to the orphans in their care.

After the August 17 blasts, five foreign officials of the RIHS left the country under pressure from the government. Before joining the RIHS they had worked for the Al-Haramain in Bangladesh.[18] The RIHS was operating in Bangladesh even after its registration was cancelled.[19]

Some Western Islamic charities have also been found to be involved in terror financing in Bangladesh. This became evident in March 2009 when a madrassa in Bhola in southern Bangladesh was raided by an anti-terrorist division, which turned up 10 firearms, 2,500 rounds of ammunition and radical Islamic literature.[20] Investigations revealed that the madrassa was funded by the British-registered charity Green Crescent, and that the founder, a British citizen Dr Faisal Mostafa, had close links with the JMB and its current leader, Saidur Rahman.[21] This charity is funded by the Bangladeshi diaspora. The Green Crescent case highlights the lack of oversight by the authorities—in Britain as well as in Bangladesh. It also proved beyond doubt that some of the Islamic NGOs are a major source of funding for militant groups. As there is no clarity regarding the number of local NGOs it is difficult to monitor and regulate them.

Use of Funds in Terror Attacks

The JMB is implementing plans originally hatched by AHAB and the HuJI. The organisation had an elaborate structure when Abdur Rahman and Bangla Bhai were leading it. In 2004 the JMB chief Abdur Rahman disclosed that he had a network of 10,000 full-time trained operatives and 100,000 part-time activists, which required more than $10,000 a month to run. The JMB was spending in 2005 roughly Tk 60 lakh a year for maintaining its leaders and cadres, and Tk 1 to 5 crore for buying explosives and firearms and executing attacks.[22] A high-ranking JMB cadre disclosed that he was spending Tk 46,000 to Tk 50,000 a month to run his regional network encompassing four districts. In year 2006, JMB had recruited special suicide bombers for the Shahid Nasirullah Arafat Brigade, who were getting monthly salaries while in training and their families were promised Tk 50,000 to 1 lakh or more in compensation after the "act of martyrdom."[23]

After the August 2005 serial bomb blasts the Bangladesh Bank asked the commercial banks of the country to send detailed information about the bank accounts of Maulana Fariduddin Masud, ex-director of Islamic Foundation who was detained for his suspected link with the 17 August bombings and his organisation the Isla-hul Muslemin Parishad. The security agencies found three crore taka in three accounts of Maulana Masud. He had withdrawn Tk 70 lakh in the month of June which it is suspected was used for the bomb blasts of 17 August.[24]

Release of RIHS funds was suspended after the arrests of Galib, and Samad Salafi in February 2005. Its regional director general for Asia, Abu Khaled Falah Al Mutairee and its country director general, Abdul Aziz Khalaf Maalullah, both Kuwaiti citizens, visited Bangladesh for six days. They met high-ranking leaders of the BNP led ruling alliance, leaders of AHAB, and some officials of the Kuwait Embassy, the NGO bureau, and of several other Middle Eastern NGOs. They convinced the government to release the fund. The government did not even conduct any spot-investigation of the projects funded by the organisation.

As a result of this lobbying the government consented to release about Tk 2 crore to the Bangladesh branch of RIHS which was immediately followed by the carnage on two court premises on 29 November.[25] On the same day, the RIHS started distributing funds among its contractors but through bearer cheques, making it easier for just about anyone to withdraw money from the bank.

Islamic NGOs get Support of Islamist Coalition Partners

While the Islamist NGOs that have funded terror might have hidden their illegal activities well, a more important reason for these outfits being able to carry on their work is that such funding has the backing of powerful sections within Bangladesh. The former four-party coalition government led by the center-right Bangladesh Nationalist Party (BNP) included the fundamentalist Jamaat-e-Islami and the Islami Oikya Jote. Several leaders of the Jamaat and the Islami Oikya Jote are known to have links with terror groups such as the JMB and the Jagrata Muslim Janata, Bangladesh (JMJB).

The former Bangladesh Nationalist Party (BNP) led four-party coalition was critical of the non-Islamic NGOs from the very beginning, but did nothing to check the funding of Islamic NGOs. The BNP itself might not be supporting the terror outfits but by appeasing its allies and ignoring the activity of their terrorist friends, it had indirectly allowed extremists to function easily. It was not that Bangladeshi security agencies were not aware of the links between the Islamist NGOs and the terror outfits but that they were under orders to ignore it. There are also close links between local police and the extremists.

Investment: Attempt of Islamist Organisations to Become Self-Reliant

While foreign funds channelled through Islamist NGOs are an important part of jihadi financing, terror organisations are however becoming increasingly self-reliant. They are reportedly running business ventures and have invested in transport, pharmaceutical companies, financial institutions and real estate.[26]

Abul Barkat, a Bangladesh economist believes that beside the regular inflow of funds from abroad, extremist outfits now earn an annual net income of about $ 200 million. The highest share of such profits come from financial institutions (banks, insurance companies, leasing companies, etc.). The other major contributors are the income coming from NGOs, trading concerns, pharmaceuticals and healthcare related institutions including diagnostic centres, educational institutions, real estate, transport, and from the news media and IT sectors.[27] It is believed that with the help of this growing Islamist economy, the Jamaat is trying to build up economic power to achieve its objective of gaining political power over time. Unlike the two main political parties, the Jamaat works with longterm plans. They have infiltrated the administration, bureaucracy, the army, media and increasingly, even NGOs. The Jamaat also controls the largest bank, the Islamic Bank of Bangladesh, six universities throughout the country, and a think tank in Dhaka.

According to Khulna police Islamist militants have invested in a large number of shrimp farms, under fake names and have a good number of cold storage facilities in the south-western region. Some believe that the Jamaat is rapidly growing in the poorest rural areas and fundamentalists are infiltrating every professional space, creating the "backdrop for the introduction of the strict Sharia laws."[28]

Funding Through Individuals

Individuals have also been financing terror in Bangladesh. The most important among these was Bin Laden. Laden's close associate Enam Arnot and his organisation the Benevolence International Organisation, which was registered with the NGO Bureau, had bank accounts in Bangladesh. A UN report said he was a top fund raiser for Laden. A Pakistani citizen Mohammad Sajid, who was arrested for attacking the poet Shamsur Rahman on 18 January 1999, told the police that he received Tk 2 crore and gave it to someone called Bakhtiar. Bakhtiar, when arrested in Sirajganj the same year, confessed to police that he distributed the money among 421 madrassas for training HuJI cadres. Both the militants said Laden had sponsored the development of the madrassa infrastructure.[29]

Three Bangladeshis, who were deported to Dhaka from Seoul in April 2004, collected about $87,000 and sent the money to the Jamaat in

Bangladesh. The three were members of a Seoul-based Islamic Organisation, Dawatul Islam.[30]

The countrywide bombings of 17 August 2005 were, in part, funded by two British nationals Abdur Rahman and Sajjad, who gave 10,000 pounds to JMB supremo at his hideout in Basabo. This was revealed in a confessional statement made by Mohammad Awal and Ataur Rahman Sunny, the son-in-law and younger brother of the JMB supremo Sheikh Abdur Rahman respectively, before a magistrate in Dhaka on 8 February 2008. Awal was the operations-in-charge of northern region and bought arms, ammunition, explosives and bomb-making materials with the forex sent by Abdur Rahman from London. Sunny took the responsibility of collecting explosives while Awal was assigned the job of procuring detonators and other deadly materials for the mission.[31]

Money Laundering

Militant organisations also bring in funds by money laundering. Earlier, financial institutions in Lahore and Karachi were the main distributors of the terror funds flowing into Bangladesh. But after the Pakistan government imposed some control on these institutions, funds are now coming to Bangladesh in the form of Hundis through Jessore, Chittagong and Dhaka.[32] Though money laundering is not synonymous with terror financing, but nonetheless, the terrorist groups are beneficiaries of incomes that are generated in part from illegal transfer of money through Hundi, illegal dealings in drugs, small arms and corruption.

Remittances from expatriate Bangladeshis working in the Middle East, the United Kingdom and elsewhere are a further area of concern. Currently estimated at $12 billion a year through banks, remittances surged from only $2 billion in 2006 as a result of financial institutions improving their delivery time and including value-added services. A further $7 billion, however, is estimated to enter Bangladesh illegally through the hundi system, an illegal alternative remittance system similar to the hawala network that operates in the Middle East. The Bangladesh government is loathe to legalize hundi—which would increase oversight—as it would divert capital away from the official banking sector and the financial system.

Besides, a section of Islamic scholars, leaders of religion-based political parties including the Jamaat and heads of madrassas go to Middle Eastern countries every year for fund-raising from *zakat, fitra* and individual donations in the name of religious education, charitable organisations and orphanages. There is no official record of this money as it does not come through official channels. The persons concerned carry the money themselves or send it through unofficial channels like hundi. Some exporters and importers in Dhaka and Chittagong also help in transferring the money. The foreign funds that are channelled through businessmen mainly come via Bangkok and Singapore.

This is one of the major sources of funds for the local Islamic NGOs and qaumi madrassas which do not have government recognition. The income and expenditure of these madrassas is not accounted for as they are not accountable to any government body.

Earlier, these qaumi madrassas were fully dependent on donations from the local religious elite but since the 1980s money has started coming in from the oil-rich Middle East countries. As a result, more than 10,000 madrassas have sprung up across the country. A large portion of the funds collected for the qaumi madrassas is allegedly used for arms training as part of preparations for 'jihad'. A number of Bangladeshi returnees from Afghan war also operate such madrassas and charitable organisations with foreign funds. One such returnee formed an Islamic NGO and also became a legislator as the nominee of a religion-based party, which was a constituent of the four-party ruling alliance.

In March 2007, Ann Peterson, assistant secretary for International Narcotics and Law Enforcement Affairs, released a report in Washington on the money laundering and terrorist financing situation in Bangladesh. The report recommended that the Bangladesh's anti-money laundering/terrorist financing regimes should be strengthened to comply with international standards. It also suggested that Bangladesh should criminalise terrorist finance and make individual bankers responsible for money laundering by their institutions.[33]

The report however admitted that while there is evidence of funds laundered through the official banking system, there is no indication of large-scale abuse. The report also indicated that principal money laundering vulnerability lies outside the formal banking system, and the underground "hawala" or "hundi" system was used to transfer money and value informally. The vast majority of hundi transactions in Bangladesh are used to repatriate wages from Bangladeshi workers abroad.

The report felt that:

> Hundi, however, will probably never be completely eradicated as it is used to avoid taxes, customs duties and currency controls. The non-convertibility of the local currency (the taka) coupled with intense

> scrutiny on foreign currency transactions in formal financial institutions also contribute to the popularity of both hundi and black market money exchanges.[34]

The report pointed out that:

> In Bangladesh, hundi primarily uses trade goods to provide counter valuation or a method of balancing the books in transactions. It is part of trade-based money laundering and a compensation mechanism for the significant amount of goods smuggled into Bangladesh. An estimated $1 billion dollars worth of dutiable goods are smuggled every year from India into Bangladesh. A comparatively small amount of goods are smuggled out of the country into India. Instead, hard currency and other assets flow out of Bangladesh to support the smuggling networks.[35]

Bangladesh is a member of the Asia Pacific Group on Money Laundering (APG). The APG initiative aims to ensure that proceeds from crime do not infiltrate the economy. They also address the issue of terrorism financing.[36] In August 2008, a five-member expert team from the APG evaluated the country's safeguards against money laundering and terror finances. David Shannon, the head of the APG delegation felt Bangladesh needed mechanisms to identify suspicious bank transactions so that they can be tracked through proper investigations.[37]

The world's lone anti-money laundering organisation, Financial Action Task Force (FATF) in a draft report to the government, has observed that "Bangladesh faces significant risk of money laundering and some risk of terrorism financing." It also suggested that Bangladesh should amend money laundering laws to plug the loopholes that allow international transactions in drug trade, terror finance and corruption. The report lauds the recent steps taken by the government but observes that there are still some deficiencies. In response to this report, the Bangladesh government agreed to amend two of the anti-money laundering laws and improve its capacity to detect financial crimes.

Bangladesh has a cash-based economy and bank transactions and bulk cash smuggling are most common methods of laundering. It is a common phenomenon in Bangladesh for sending illegal money abroad. The vulnerability to terror finance stem from foreign remittances sent in the name of charities and the use of cash couriers. The loose control over NGOs is also a cause of concern. The cash based nature of Bangladesh economy also underlines the need to closely monitor courier services, micro-finance institutions, money changers, money remittance/ fund transfer companies, post offices, real estate agencies etc. through which money can reach terrorist groups.[38]

Role of Financial Institutions

Bangladesh has the largest number of banks in South Asia with 47 local and foreign banks in the country. Besides this, the Bangladesh Bank has received 37 applications for permission to set up new banks.[39] Such a large number inevitably raises suspicion. Many of these banks are suspected to be involved in the laundering of terrorist funds received and further transmitting them through hawala (informal money transfer) networks. The banks also heavily subsidise madrassa education, fund the construction of mosques and contribute towards the Haj.

In February 2011, Shamsul Hoque Tuku, the home state minister alleged that the Islami Bank spends around eight per cent of its profit to finance militants. He revealed that the bank was transferring "funds from the bank to the Islami Bank Foundation."[40] The bank was spending more than Tk. 25 crore on such activities. This was for the first time that a source of terror funding has been identified by the government.[41] Though the bank refuted the allegation, the Bangladesh Bank warned Islamic banks against indulging in terror financing, money laundering or any other illegal activities that could damage their image.[42]

Both Bangladeshi NGOs as well as the state prefer Saudi and general Islamic funding to multilateral lending. Japan is Bangladesh's largest donor followed by the US and EU, but the country is not keen on this aid, because post-utilisation certificates are required to be submitted. Saudi funding, on the other hand, is directly to individuals, which permits huge leaks.[43]

Dismal Record of Bangladesh Bank in Checking Terror Finance

The Bangladesh Bank has received approximately 236 suspicious transaction reports since the Money Laundering Prevention Act (MLPA) was enacted in 2002. To date, there have been no successful prosecutions, in part due to procedural problems in adjusting to inter-agency cooperation. A major setback occurred in December 2005 when the Anti-Corruption Commission (ACC) advised the bank that it would not investigate these cases and returned them.[44]

According to some bank officials it was really very difficult to trace any source of terror financing under the existing system, as the Bangladesh Bank depends mainly on its banking-related information. However, some other officials were of opinion that high officials and the directors of some banks were involved in the transactions of money used to fund terrorist activities and if the Bangladesh Bank and the intelligence agencies were to choose to investigate these suspects, the fund channelling should not be too tough to trace. Still others claimed the bank has many limitation as well as systemic loopholes that hamper it in detecting and checking such suspicious transactions.[45]

The Bangladesh Bank is struggling to implement regulations, because it lacks the manpower and finances to investigate foreign and domestic transactions passing through the financial system. Bank officials concede that some of the country's six Islamic banks are "not properly run." The country equally lacks reporting agencies, relating to car dealerships and precious stones, raising concerns that such businesses could be used to launder money and finance terrorism.[46]

Fake Currency

In recent times, Bangladesh has become a major source of fake currency directed for India. Earlier Bangladesh was only a transit route for fake currency but now reports have indicated that the fake currency is being printed in that country and then dumped into India. Evidence has emerged indicating that Chapai Nawabgunj is one of many centres in Bangladesh where counterfeit Indian notes are printed. The fake currency printing unit here was being operated by a Bangladesh Nationalist Party leader who allegedly has links with Pakistan's Inter-Services Intelligence (ISI).[47] Over the past couple of years, Malda and adjoining Murshidabad have become important transit points through which high-denomination fake currency notes are smuggled in for "distribution" and eventual circulation in the Indian market.[48] During the four-party regime the BSF did not get much cooperation from the BDR but now under the present Sheikh Hasina regime the Bangladesh border-guards are cooperating with India.[49]

The arrest of four men including three Kashmiris by the West Bengal police in 2008 indicated that the fake currency racket operating out of Bangladesh was channelling funds to terrorist groups like the LeT) to carry out subversive activities across India.[50] The extent of this menace became clear after seizures of huge amount of FICN worth crores of rupees from agents working closely with the perpetrators of the twin blasts in Hyderabad. Police had seized Rs 2.36 crores days before the serial blasts which prompted the home ministry to take up this issue with the external affairs and finance ministries.[51]

Drugs

Islamist organisations the world over have used drug trade as a major source of funding.[52] Bangladesh is no exception. In 2004 the British authorities first found out about the heroin smuggling and arrested 12 UK citizens of Bangladeshi origin. Most of these people were from Sylhet and were subsequently imprisoned.[53]

In 2005 a five-member probe committee formed by the National Board of Revenue detected that five Bangladeshi business companies were involved in smuggling heroin into the UK. The board initiated the enquiry after the UK customs in a message through the British mission in Mumbai accused King and Company, a sister concern of BD Foods Limited, Emdad Traders, Jamil International, MM Enterprise, and Green Heaven Enterprise of trafficking 75.5 kilograms of heroin to the UK. It was also learnt from the interrogation that a major portion of the profit accruing from the trafficking in narcotics went for funding Islamist terrorist groups within Bangladesh and outside. A US report also mentions that 140 kg of heroin was brought into the United Kingdom as part of several shipments originating from the Chittagong port in Bangladesh.[54]

The report prepared by the FATF also suggested that Bangladesh is a trans-shipment point for illegal drugs bound for markets in Europe, the US and Canada. The report notes, "The majority of illegal proceeds of crime in Bangladesh stem from trafficking of illicit drugs, human trafficking and corruption."

Underworld

The militant Islamic groups of Bangladesh have also received funding from the underworld. A militant terror organisation Shahadat-e-Al-Hikma (SAH) was launched in 1997 but started its activities openly in 2001 as an NGO. The convener of Al-Hikma, Kawsar Hossain Siddique, while announcing its launch on 8 February 2002 had said that the outfit was financed by Dawood Ibrahim, who heads the list of most-wanted terrorists in India. This organisation was however banned after a powerful bomb blast at a religious institution in northern Dinajpur. This was the first crackdown on an extremist Islamic outfit by the Khaleda Zia government. But it had rejected the demand made by Suranjit Sen Gupta, of the Awami League, who called for the formation of a parliamentary committee to probe into the source of funding and arms flow into such terrorist outfits.[55]

Role of International Community/UN

The United States became concerned about rising Islamic militancy in Bangladesh after 9/11. Under US pressure Bangladesh enacted the Money Laundering Prevention Act (MLPA), 2002. But this law was not very effective in checking terror finance. The US kept pressurising Bangladesh to enact an improved law in line with its strategy to combat global terrorist activities. The four-party alliance government kept resisting this pressure because the Jamaat was part of the government. However things improved during the regime of second caretaker government and during the second tenure of Sheikh Hasina.

The US has been engaged in training top bureaucrats and bankers of Bangladesh in investigating terror financing and money laundering.[56] In March 2006 the US sent Treasury Department's Financial Crimes Enforcement Network (FinCEN) Senior Research Analyst Mary Jo Melancon and Senior Intelligence Research Specialist Kristen J King to Bangladesh to acquaint a select group of police, judicial, customs and central bank officials with the methods used by FinCEN to safeguard the US financial system from abuses and crimes like terrorist financing and money laundering.[57]

Bangladesh is now a party to 12 UN conventions and protocols on terrorism. In 2005, the government became a party to the UN International Convention for the Suppression of the Financing of Terrorism. Now Bangladesh is seeking to strengthen the monitoring of bank accounts and fund transactions to detect terrorism financing effectively. Besides, it will help prevent illegal money transfers through the banking channels. If necessary, Bangladesh will also seek international cooperation in this regard.

Attitude of Government Towards Terrorist Financing

The attitude of the Bangladesh government towards checking terror financing varies according to the regime in power. The four-party coalition which was in power since 2001 adopted a half-hearted approach. It did not feel any need to enforce a stringent law as it would have affected its coalition partners the Jamaat and the IOJ. The government was under pressure after 9/11 which prompted it to enact the MLPA, 2002 which made the Bangladesh Bank responsible for overseeing financial institutions and ensuring that customer activities are adequately monitored and suspicious transactions followed up.[58] Unfortunately, the MLPA did not prove very effective. Both the finance ministry and the Bangladesh Bank believed that the ordinance was formulated hurriedly under pressure from the USA. The main flaw of the act was that it did not specify what kind of crimes falls under its purview. It also did not specify who would investigate the cases filed under this act or which institutions are supposed to act as its watchdogs. These loopholes in the law made it meaningless.[59]

Bangladesh's army-backed interim government however approved a new counter-terrorism law, laying down a maximum penalty of death for anyone involved in terrorist activities. The council of advisers (cabinet) chaired by government head Fakhruddin Ahmed approved the ordinance on 18 May 2008 that also provides for "speedy trial of terrorists by special courts", with jail sentences ranging from three to 20 years. The ordinance says that anyone responsible for "financing terrorist groups, whether local or foreign, will also be tried under the anti-terrorism law and a convict will serve maximum 20 years of rigorous imprisonment or minimum three years with financial penalty."[60] Bangladesh Bank will have the authority to identify monetary transactions through banking channel for terror funding.[61] Previously Bangladesh had no separate law for dealing with terrorists. They were instead tried under the normal penal code.

In February 2009, the Awami League-led government passed the Money Laundering Prevention Act (MLPA), and the Anti-terrorism Act (ATA). Although not fully compliant with international standards, the MLPA addressed many flaws in the preceding 2002 money laundering law while the ATA for the first time enabled the Bangladesh legal system to deal with terrorist financing. The laws facilitate international cooperation and a Financial Intelligence Unit (FIU) was set up at the Bangladesh Bank. The new laws are part of the effort to enable Bangladesh to gain access to the Egmont Group, the international body of FIUs, that plays a critical role in fighting terrorist financing.[62]

In 2010, the government tried to implement these provisions, and examined further areas for legislative improvements to the Money Laundering Prevention Act and the Anti-Terrorism Act, actions that reflected Bangladesh's receptivity to international peer review mechanisms and the Financial Action Task Force (FATF) International Cooperation Review Group process. In November, the government established the National Coordination Committee, comprised of all agencies dealing with the anti-money laundering/countering terrorist finance issue, to provide operational level coordination and to develop a national strategy.

The international establishments like FATF and Asia Pacific Group (APG) had been pressing the government to incorporate the offences such as financial crimes into the Extradition act. Similar suggestion was made by the Justice Department of the US government and even the finance ministry of Bangladesh. Keeping these in view the Hasina government showed its desire to deal with terrorist financing and money laundering and amended the schedule of the Extradition Act, 1974 to help bring back from abroad the Bangladeshi fugitives involved in money laundering and financing of terrorist activities. The home ministry on 14 February 2011 added two new clauses to the schedule of the act through a gazette notification covering crimes such as money laundering and financing of terrorist activities.

Bangladesh has also submitted its time-bound action plan to FATF to prevent money laundering and terrorist financing. The finance ministry also formed a 12-member National Coordination Committee, headed by Finance Minister AMA Muhith, to implement the FATF road map.

Financing of Indian Insurgent Groups Based in Bangladesh

Extortion

The Northeast insurgent groups like the Naga National Council, the NSCN or the Mizo National Front (MNF) were in their early days careful not to disturb civic life. They secured arms by ambushing army or police personnel and taking their arms. They also used to coerce government employees, professionals and businessmen, locals or outsiders into paying a certain amount of money as 'tax' to the government-in-exile which covered their maintenance expenses.

But from the 1990s there has been radical transformation in the character of Northeast insurgency. Extortion, abduction and looting of treasuries have become common. Besides tea gardens, public sector units like ONGC, OIL, NEEPCO and even the Indian railways have to regularly shell out substantial amounts as protection money.

Two major NSCN factions in Nagaland are currently in ceasefire mode, and reports of extortions are frequent. There have been reports of government employees paying "tax" according to their pay scale. Though not many statistics are available as most extortion cases go unreported, with traders and individuals preferring to pay up rather than invite trouble, the police in Dimapur—Nagaland's trade hub—registered as many as 162 extortion cases in 2009, mostly filed by truck drivers and transport operators. "Tax" on trucks carrying onions is between Rs 8,000 and Rs 9,000; those carrying steel pay Rs 12,000; and those carrying medicines up to Rs 25,000.[63]

The worst hit however is Manipur where the insurgency has really proliferated in recent times and which has the largest number of underground outfits in the country. While the NSCN (IM), whose general secretary hails from Ukhrul district in Manipur, allegedly collects anywhere between Rs 20 and 30 crores from Manipur, all other groups also heavily depend upon extortion to run their organisations. Thus "tax" is imposed on traders, transporters, suppliers, contractors and government as well as private employees, hospitals and educational institutions. Conservative estimates put the total sum drained away through extortions at about Rs 100 crore per year.

In Assam, despite the stock of ULFA being at an all-time low (chairman Arabinda Rajkhowa and most top leaders are in jail), the outfit is said to be still collecting about Rs 10 crores a month, mostly from tea companies, traders and contractors. Similarly, though the National Democratic Front of Bodoland (NDFB) has split and its founder chairman Ranjan Daimary is in jail, its cadres continue to extort money in several districts, including Guwahati. In the Dima Hasao (erstwhile North Cachar Hills) district, where developmental funds amounting to several hundreds of crores have been siphoned off by a nexus of militants, bureaucrats, suppliers and politicians, people still receive "tax" notice from the NSCN (IM).

Though the insurgency in Meghalaya is not as widespread as in Assam and Manipur, the state too has a huge problem of extortion. Several underground groups collect crores of rupees from traders, particularly those into coal mining. In September, 2010 a district transport officer in Garo Hills was kidnapped after he failed to respond to a notice for Rs 50 lakh from Garo National Liberation Army.

While extortion is not a major headache in Mizoram and Tripura, people in certain districts of Arunachal Pradesh are feeling the heat. Both factions of the NSCN allegedly collect about Rs 2 crores a month from traders, contractors and suppliers in Tirap and Changlang districts.

Though the space for insurgency in Northeast has been shrinking, the extortion has not abated because it has become "a cottage industry being run by the criminal gangs."[64]

Arms and Contraband Trade

In the Northeast of India, particularly Manipur, militancy has been associated with drug trafficking since the 1990s. Most of this drug comes through Indo-Myanmar border. The seriousness of trafficking was first highlighted in 1992, when ethnic conflict broke out between the armed militant groups of Nagas (NSCN) and Kuki (KNA) tribes, because each wished to control drug trafficking and smuggling in Moreh, a border town in Chandel district.

Traditionally, cross-border trafficking of drugs from Northeast India was rare and the Manipur Valley-based insurgent groups did not indulge in drug related activities. But this changed subsequently. With enhanced deployment of security forces along the Indo-Myanmar border and successful counter-insurgency operations like "Operation All Clear" which had deprived them of their bases in the remote hill areas, the militants received a setback. They are looking for new hideouts, trying to regroup and set a positive image by not indulging in extortions from the masses. This has been the reason for the militant groups such as KCP and KYKL (Kanglei Yawol Kanna Lup) to adopt drug trafficking to fund their organisation and activites. Moreover, the image and the organisational structure of the militants have become weak in recent years, especially given the loss of vital support from the masses. Numerous groups have arisen out of a single group and many are operating with sophisticated small arms in nexus with the drug mafias.

Business in Bangladesh

Some of the prominent insurgent groups in Northeast like the United Liberation Front of Asom (ULFA) have established businesses in Bangladesh and they use its profits for running insurgency. This money also supports the lavish lifestyle of their top leaders. It is believed that the lure of this money is also a major factor behind the refusal of ULFA's commander-in-chief Paresh Barua to accept the proposal of peace talks.

On 3 June 2005 Indian security forces unveiled a list of hotels and other assets owned by the ULFA in Bangladesh. The Border Security Force's top official in the Northeast, S.C. Shrivastava disclosed that ULFA leaders based in Bangladesh were managing as many as seven hotels of "international standard." Besides, they also owned some nursing homes. He alleged that the militant group owned Surma International, Hotel Mohammadia and Padma International in Dhaka, Keya International and Hotel Yamuna in Sylhet and Hotel Basundhara and Hotel Raj King in Chittagong. He said the managers of these hotels were ULFA militants who operated under aliases such as Ahmed, Kamal Hossain, Saidul, Shoal, Humayun and Rubel.

The BSF revealed details of at least three of ULFA's "active" bank accounts. The accounts were traced to Arab Bangladesh Bank's Zinda Bazaar branch in Sylhet (account number 025401/08), the same bank's Farm Gate branch in Dhaka (account number 5266709/15) and Al-barakah Bank's Pahartali branch in Chittagong (account number 09/229472).

Dhaka, on its part, took virtually no time in denying the BSF claim of ULFA's business interests in Bangladesh. IG Abdul Quayum of Bangladesh

Police said, "We don't have any such information." The foreign ministry also categorically denied the report that the United Liberation Front of Assam (Ulfa) runs hotels and operates bank accounts in Bangladesh.

In September 2011, Indian intelligence agencies prepared a detailed report with graphic details about Baruah's investments and income. This report talked of Baruah's investments in real estate, the health sector, textiles, shipping, power projects and restaurants. Baruah invested over $20 million in various companies in Bangladesh under false identities. Of this, $14 million was pumped into three Dhaka-based real estate firms—Basundhara Real Estate, Eastern Housing Project and Jamuna Group Housing Project—under the name of Karujjaman, a London businessman. In Basundhara, Baruah has a 17 per cent stake with an investment of $7 million; while in Eastern Housing he has a nine per cent stake with an investment of $4 million; while in Jamuna he has a two per cent stake by investing $3 million.

Under the name of Jumen, a businessman from Dubai, Baruah has invested $200,000 in Samrita Hospital, Dhaka, in which he has 30 per cent. The hospital is owned by one Dr Jahid Hassan. In Kasem Textiles, owned by AKM Maidul Islam, Baruah has a 30 per cent stake with an investment of $1.7 million. In Chowdhury Shipping he has a 30 per cent stake with an investment of $2.5 million. Baruah also has a 40 per cent share in Dhaka's famous Chinese restaurant, Wimfray, in which he invested $100,000. Dhaka has now assured New Delhi it will crack down on these outfits.

Notes

1. Tim Parkman and Gill Peeling, *Countering Terrorist Finance*, Gower Publishing Limited, England, 2007, pp. 23-24. For a detailed discussion of the subject please also see, Anand Kumar, "Terror Financing in Bangladesh," *Strategic Analysis*, Vol. 33, No. 6, November 2009, 903–917
2. William P. Fuller and Barnett F. Baron, "How war on terror hits charity," *The Christian Science Monitor*, Boston, July 29, 2003 http://www.csmonitor.com/2003/0729/p11s01-coop.html?entryBottomStory
3. USA PATRIOT Act, at http://www.fincen.gov/statutes_regs/patriot/index.html
4. Jeremy Scott-Joynt, "Charities in Terror Fund Spotlight," *BBC News*, 15 October, 2003, at http://news.bbc.co.uk/2/hi/business/3186840.stm
5. "Saudi government moves to tighten control of charities," The *USA Today*, 06 February 2004, at http://www.usatoday.com/news/world/2004-06-02-saudi-charities_x.htm
6. Ibid.
7. "Saudi Ban on Islamic Militant: Al-Haramain continues operation in Bangladesh," *The Daily Star*, 04 June, 2004 at http://www.thedailystar.net/2004/06/04/d4060401055.htm
8. Ibid.
9. "Foreign funds channelled to Bangladesh for Jihad cause," *The China Daily*, September 06, 2005, at http://english.people.com.cn/200509/06/eng20050906_206886.html
10. Ibid.

11. "34 Islamic NGOs get over Tk 200cr from donors a year," *The Daily Star*, August 31, 2005, http://www.thedailystar.net/2005/08/31/d5083101044.htm
12. "Foreign funds channelled to Bangladesh for Jihad cause," September 06, 2005, *People's Daily* Online, Beijing at http://english.people.com.cn/200509/06/eng20050906_206886.html
13. "NGOs under scanner for 'funding militancy': Govt to scrutinise activities of NGOs okayed during Mojahid's stint," *The Daily Star*, 19 March 2009 at http://www.thedailystar.net/newDesign/news-details.php?nid=80287
14. "34 Islamic NGOs get over Tk 200cr from donors a year," *The Daily Sta*r, August 31, 2005, http://www.thedailystar.net/2005/08/31/d5083101044.htm
15. "Terror-financing NGOs remain unscathed," *The Daily Star*, November 26, 2005 at http://www.thedailystar.net/2005/11/26/d5112601022.htm
16. Zayadul Ahsan, "Inside the Militant Groups-2: Foreign funding, local business keep them going," the *Daily Star*, August 22, 2005 http://www.thedailystar.net/2005/08/22/d5082201044.htm
17. Sudha Ramachandran, "Mixing aid with terror," *Asia Times* Online, September 22, 2005, http://www.atimes.com/atimes/South_Asia/GI22Df01.html
18. "Terror-financing NGOs remain unscathed," *The Daily Star*, November 26, 2005, http://www.thedailystar.net/2005/11/26/d5112601022.htm
19. Anwar Ali, "Banned Kuwait-based NGO runs covertly," *The Daily Star*, 31 March 2009 at http://www.thedailystar.net/newDesign/news-details.php?nid=82101
20. Militants' 'ammo factory' busted, *The Daily Star*, March 25, 2009, at http://www.thedailystar.net/newDesign/news-details.php?nid=81208
21. "Bhola kids given lessons of jihad: Students tell investigators," *The Daily Star*, 29 March 2009 http://www.thedailystar.net/story.php?nid=81789
22. "Terror-financing NGOs remain unscathed," *The Daily Star*, November 26, 2005, http://www.thedailystar.net/2005/11/26/d5112601022.htm
23. Martin Walker, "India to warn Bush of Bangladesh terror," as accessed on March 3, 2006 at http://www.upi.com/InternationalIntelligence/view.php?StoryID=20060301-120024-9068r, Please also see Dr. Peter Snowman, "Bangladesh's open solidarity to Hamas government," *Asian Tribune*, at http://www.asiantribune.com/oldsite/show_article.php?id=3147, also see Terror-financing NGOs remain unscathed, *The Daily Star,* November 26, 2005 at http://www.thedailystar.net/2005/11/26/d5112601022.htm
24. ANM Nurul Haque, "Foreign funding for Islamist outfits," *The Daily Star*, September 04, 2005, at http://www.thedailystar.net/2005/09/04/d509041503111.htm
25. "Govt okays release of fund to 'terror funder," *The Daily Star*, December 05, 2005, http://www.thedailystar.net/2005/12/05/d5120501044.htm
26. Zayadul Ahsan, "Inside the Militant Groups-2: Foreign funding, local business keep them going," *The Daily Star*, August 22, 2005
27. Abul Barkat, "Economics of Fundamentalism and the Growth of Political Islam in Bangladesh," *Social Science Review,* The Dhaka University Studies, Part-D, Vol. 23, No. 2, December 2006, pp. 16-17.
28. Bibhuti Bhusan Nandy, "Blind Faith" *The Hindustan Times*, 6 August 2003.
29. Zayadul Ahsan, "Inside the Militant Groups-2: Foreign funding, local business keep them going," *The Daily Star*, August 22, 2005.
30. Ibid.
31. Chaitanya Chandra Halder and Shamim Ashraf, "2 Britons funded JMB to carry out bomb attacks: Say top leaders Sunny, Awal," *The Daily Star*, 9 February 2006 at http://www.thedailystar.net/2006/02/09/d6020901044.htm

32. Zayadul Ahsan, "Inside the Militant Groups-2: Foreign funding, local business keep them going," *The Daily Star*, 22 August 2005
33. *International Narcotics Control Strategy Report–2007*, Country Reports: Bangladesh, Released by the Bureau of International Narcotics and Law Enforcement Affairs, March 2007, at http://www.state.gov/p/inl/rls/nrcrpt/2007/vol2/html/80886.htm
34. Ibid.
35. Ibid.
36. "Dhaka's steps against money laundering to be checked," 18 August 2008, *The Daily Star*, http://www.thedailystar.net/story.php?nid=50842
37. "Govt committed to check laundering: APG," *bdnews24.com*, 27 August, 2008 at http://bdnews24.com/details.php?id=60757&cid=4
38. Nazmul Hasan, "Effective Use of Anti-Money Laundering Law in Countering Terrorism in Bangladesh," in Farooq Sobhan edit. *Countering Terrorism in Bangladesh*, The University Press Limited, Dhaka, 2008, p. 126.
39. Rejaul Karim Byron, "BB receives 37 applications," *The Daily Star*, 1 December 2011 at http://www.thedailystar.net/newDesign/news-details.php?nid=212405
40. "Islami bank financing militants: Tuku," *bdnews24.com*, 28 February 2011, http://www.bdnews24.com/details.php?cid=2&id=188539&hb=top
41. Brig Gen Shahedul Anam Khan, "Terrorists and terror financing," *The Daily Star*, 3 March 2011, http://www.thedailystar.net/newDesign/news-details.php?nid=176156
42. "BB warns Islamic banks," *The Daily Star*, 22 July 2011, at http://www.thedailystar.net/newDesign/news-details.php?nid=195171
43. Sudha Ramachandran, "Mixing aid with terror," *Asia Times Online*, 22 September 2005, http://www.atimes.com/atimes/South_Asia/GI22Df01.html
44. *International Narcotics Control Strategy Report–2007*, Country Reports: Bangladesh, Released by the Bureau of International Narcotics and Law Enforcement Affairs, March 2007 at http://www.state.gov/p/inl/rls/nrcrpt/2007/vol2/html/80886.htm
45. Based on Interview of some Bangladesh Bank officials (Central Bank of Bangladesh)
46. Paul Cochrane, "The Funding Methods of Bangladeshi Terrorist Groups" 15 May 2009 at http://www.ctc.usma.edu/posts/the-funding-methods-of-bangladeshi-terrorist-groups
47. Manas Banerjee, "How the (fake) money flows...," *The Statesman*, 20 November 2008 at http://www.thestatesman.net/page.arcview.php?date=2008-11-20&usrsess=6780816707857&clid=1&id=258094
48. "Fake currency racket kingpin in Bangladesh, says SOG," *The Indian Express*, 22 September 2008 at http://www.indianexpress.com/news/fake-currency-racket-kingpin-in-bangladesh-says-sog/364313/
49. Based on authors interaction with the BSF officers.
50. Soudhriti Bhabani, "Fake currency racket in Bangladesh sets police on LeT trail," *IANS*, 8 March 2008, http://www.thaindian.com/newsportal/world-news/fake-currency-racket-in-bangladesh-sets-police-on-let-trail_10025254.html
51. Pradeep Thakur & Vishwa Mohan, "Fake currency funding terror?" *The Times of India*, 29 July 2008, at http://timesofindia.indiatimes.com/Fake_currency_funding_terror/articleshow/3299610.cms
52. Rachel Ehrenfeld, "Funding Evil: How Terrorism is Financed and the Nexus of Terrorist and Criminal Organisations," in Sean S. Costaigan and David Gold edited *Terrornomics*, Ashgate Publishing Limited, England, 2007, pp 27-48.
53. "Bangladesh heroin smuggler Momen names six government officials as abettors in the crime," *Asian Tribune*, 21-05-2006 at http://www.asiantribune.com/?q=node/203
54. *International Narcotics Control Strategy Report*, Volume I, Drug and Chemical Control, United States Department of State, Bureau for International Narcotics and Law

Enforcement Affairs, March 2007, http://www.state.gov/documents/organisation/81446.pdf, p. 234.

55. "Bangladesh cracks down on Dawood-funded extremist outfit," *The Statesman*, February 18, 2003 Please also see "Banned Islamist outfit calls press conference," *The Daily Star*, November 4, 2004, at http://www.thedailystar.net/2004/11/04/d41104012222.htm
56. "US Providing Training to Bureaucrats and Bankers in Terror Financing Probe: FBI to train up bureaucrats, bankers in terror financing probe," *New Age*, Dhaka, August 28, 2005 at http://www.newagebd.com/2005/aug/28/front.html
57. "Routing Terror Finance: Top US agency men join fight: BB, cops clueless about militants' funding sources," *The Daily Star*, March 09, 2006 at http://www.thedailystar.net/2006/03/09/d60309010l1.htm
58. Money Laundering Prevention Act,2002, Anti-Money Laundering Department, Bangladesh Bank at http://www.bangladesh-bank.org/mediaroom/circulars/aml/may1802aml01e.pdf.
59. Rejaul Karim Byron, "Move on to make BB more powerful: Finance to seek change in Anti-Money Laundering Act," March 19, 2007, http://www.thedailystar.net/2007/03/19/d70319011814.htm
60. "Bangladesh adopts tough law to curb terrorism," *Reuters*, May 19, 2008 http://www.reuters.com/article/latestCrisis/idUSDHA314301
61. "Anti-terror ordinance okayed: Death penalty provision for offenders, patrons," *The Daily Star*, 19 May 2008, http://www.thedailystar.net/pf_story.php?nid=37211
62. Bangladesh: 2009 country report on terrorism, banglanews24.com at http://www.banglanews24.com/English/detailsnews.php?nssl=9c10d235bc6941125446942ec2c0d999&nttl=2011120726092
63. Samudra Gupta Kashyap, "Northeast's worst-kept secret: Extortion rackets," The Indian Express, 1 Dec 2010, at http://www.indianexpress.com/news/northeasts-worstkept-secret-extortion-rackets/718390/0
64. NE insurgency is like a cottage industry: Pillai, *The Sentinel,* http://www.sentinelassam.com/meghalaya/story.php?sec=2&subsec=8&id=87783&dtP=2011-08-30&ppr=1

7

From Denial to Action Against Terror

The political development in Bangladesh since its liberation has ensured that the country has a constituency that supports political Islam. A section of this constituency is also militant and believes in violent methods to achieve their avowed objective of Islamic state in Bangladesh. The result of this development was that Bangladesh continued to move against the international opinion which had decisively turned against terrorism after 9/11. After the attack on twin towers, terrorist outfits were no longer tolerated. The US had come to Afghanistan to fight the war against terror with Taliban. It was successful in unseating Taliban though the war still continues. In Bangladesh during this period the centre right BNP was in power with three other parties, two of whom were Islamist groups. In fact, the IOJ openly showed its allegiance to al-Qaeda. Jamaat despite having small number of MPs exercised great control over the administration. It was said that in the four-party alliance government, tail was wagging the dog. Though the terrorism entered Bangladesh during this period in a big way the BNP led government chose to either ignore or underplay the issue.

While the extremist groups openly talked about their objective of establishing an Islamic state the BNP led government pretended ignorance. Jamaat-e-Islami functions as a political party, but it shares the end objective with the militant Islamist groups, i.e. of establishing an Islamic state. The only difference between Jamaat and other extremist groups is that Jamaat wants to completely Islamise society before opting for Islamic state so that it is enduring. It was very clear that the democracy in Bangladesh was under stress during four-party alliance rule and extremist elements were trying to bring changes in it so that soon it would become impossible for the secular parties like Awami League to function and come to power.

It is not surprising then during the BNP regime Bangladesh continued to deny the existence of Islamist forces and when it became impossible to deny this existence it actually defended them. The same approach also made them see Indian insurgents as "freedom fighters".

Awami League remained out of power till 1996 and even when they were in power from 1996–2001 they had a thin majority. However, things drastically changed when Sheikh Hasina came to power after the October 2008 elections. In this election, the party got overwhelming majority. The government has now gone all out against terror.

Soft/Dubious Approach of the BNP on Terror

The Islamist militants had grown in strength during the first tenure of the BNP led government from 1991-96. They became further strong when the BNP came back to power in 2001. During the second tenure of the BNP led government Jamaat and IOJ were parts of the ruling coalition. Though their support was not needed for the survival of the government, Khaleda Zia and her party did not do anything to check the activity of Jamaat. In fact, Jamaat was rewarded with two very crucial ministries through which it tried to Islamise the country by following certain policies. Though a section in the BNP was uneasy in the company of Jamaat, the top BNP leadership saw political advantages of keeping Jamaat on their side.

The overwhelming influence of Jamaat on administration ensured that no meaningful action would be taken against extremist elements, who were seen to be offshoots of Jamaat. Jamaat was able to manipulate the administration with ease as it has made inroads in the government's security machinery at all levels with the help of the largest political party, BNP in the ruling coalition. Even the Home Secretary Muhammad Omar Farooq was widely regarded as close to the Jamaat. Many feared that the Jamaat and its allies have penetrated the higher ranks of the armed forces. It was suspected that Maj. Gen. Mohammed Aminul Karim, appointed as military secretary to President Iajuddin Ahmed, and to Brig. Gen. A.T.M. Amin, director of the Armed Forces Intelligence anti-terrorism bureau are linked to Jamaat.

The influence of BNP's alliance with Jamaat was also seen in its policies towards Islamist groups. It was very difficult for the BNP to acknowledge the existence of such forces in Bangladesh and take action against them while being in company of Jamaat and IOJ. For a long time, BNP continued to deny the presence of extremists in the country.

The increasing activity of Islamists and deteriorating law and order condition in Bangladesh however created worldwide concern. It was feared that if things are not controlled in Bangladesh then the country might also become another trouble-spot like Pakistan or Afghanistan. This concern of the international community made them think of ways to put pressure on Bangladesh to check extremist activities.

Pressure Through Bangladesh Development Forum (BDF)

In a least developed country like Bangladesh the making of annual development plans (ADP) depends on money coming from the donors. Though matters have improved in recent times, the country still remains dependent on foreign aid.

The Bangladesh Development Forum (BDF) consists of about 40 leading donors including: the Asian Development Bank (ADB), the European Union (EU), Germany, Japan, the US and the UK. However, in the BDF meetings during the four-party alliance rule, Bangladesh had to face uncomfortable questions relating to poor governance, corruption, and the deteriorating law and order situation. The donors were also frustrated by the inaction of the government on the human rights and terrorism fronts. The donors wanted aid to be linked to "greater response to good governance and human rights and restraining militants, all issues of serious international concerns".

In 2005 Bangladesh donors decided to meet in Washington on 23-24 February. They also did not invite any officials from Bangladesh which raised hackles in Bangladesh. The Bangladesh government went into a high-lobbying mode. The government sent Reaz Rahman, adviser in the foreign ministry to the US where he met Christina Rocca the assistant secretary of state for South Asia. During the meeting Rocca expressed her concern about the militancy, political turmoil, grenade attacks on the opposition leaders and the government inaction to check the situation. Reaz assured the US government that steps would be taken against the Islamist militants.

Finance Minister M Saifur Rahman went to Brussels in a bid to persuade the EU to review its stance.[1] He met 13 EU commissioners and conveyed his concerns about the Washington meeting to the EU external affairs commissioner. Saifur felt that the meeting could have been held in Bangladesh or at least its representatives could have been invited. He also accused the opposition of feeding the EU with wrong information about Bangladesh. He believed that this created an unhealthy attitude among some European countries about Bangladesh. Hence they were not looking at Bangladesh from an appropriate perspective.

The Washington meeting was jointly organised by the World Bank, the EU and the US state department. A large group of European donors wanted the donors and the US to take a tough line on aid and link it with good governance, human rights and anti terror measures. They believed that the Bangladesh government had been too lenient towards militants, which had led to a spate of armed attacks and killings. They were also concerned by the failure of the government to solve any of the political killings that had taken place around that time. They wanted the World Bank (WB), the Asian Development Bank (ADB) and the US to rethink their financial assistance to Bangladesh. They felt that the two donors with the highest stake in Bangladesh had not been sufficiently vocal about these threats but were focused only on the positive macroeconomic indicators. The World Bank and Asian Development Bank however were of the view that a tough approach would be counterproductive and throw the country into a deeper turmoil.

But the Washington meet was successful in one respect. It forced the Bangladesh government to indirectly admit to the existence of Islamic extremists. Though, the government remained in denial mode, Bangladesh in a small crackdown arrested some local level Islamist leaders just before the donors' meeting in Washington but left the prominent leaders of Islamist groups untouched. Bangladesh also banned the JMB and the JMJB on 23 February 2005. But these cosmetic measures ended with the donor meeting.

BNP and Jamaat Leaders Revert to Hostility After Donor Meet

Bangladeshi leaders were angered by pressure exerted by the donor community. Both Prime Minister Khaleda Zia and Finance Minister M Saifur Rahman asked the donors to leave if they could not accept the policies and economic programmes of the country. Saifur Rahman said, "The donors have to align with our policy, not us with theirs."[2] He accused the donors of "interfering with the internal politics of Bangladesh." He also pointed out that Bangladesh was now no longer dependent on foreign aid as it had been immediately after its liberation. Referring to an earlier aid meeting in Paris he said that he had asked the donors to agree to 'performance-based aid, rather than condition-based one.'[3]

While speaking in Bangladesh parliament on 15 March 2005, Prime Minister, Khalida Zia warned the donor agencies and foreign nations against interfering in the country's domestic affairs. What was most surprising was that she also denied the existence of any Islamist militancy or religious extremism in the country. She denied the existence of Taliban and al-Qaeda elements in Bangladesh. She claimed that: "It's a propaganda against the government and the country. And it is aimed at causing a rift within the four-party alliance."[4] Referring to arrests of some people taking place at that time for their suspected involvement in Islamist militancy and religious extremism, Khaleda said, "That were not problems of extremism and fundamentalism, rather we believe those were law and order problems."[5] The prime minister also said that the Islamic organisations have long been working to spread the message of Islam and its ideology. "They've also made an important contribution to maintaining social integrity and harmony; and there's no allegation against them."

Similar remarks were made by the leaders of the Jamaat and IOJ leaders in and outside the parliament. The industries minister Nizami claimed that none of the known Islamic organisations had any links with militancy. Another law maker from the Jamaat Mia Golam Parwar in his speech in parliament on 8 March 2005 accused the Awami League of conspiring to cause a rift within the ruling alliance.

But the government was contradicting itself because it had banned the JMJB and the JMB on grounds that they were trying to create anarchy in the society by using religious sentiments to misguide the youth of the country.[6]

Government Considered Various Options to Ward-off Donor Pressure

Bangladesh considered various options to deal with the donor pressure. It wanted to fund and organise the donor meeting to take over the helm from the World Bank. In addition, it also favoured holding the meeting every two years instead of annually. The objective was to face the donors after two years rather than every year as the case was now. The BDF meetings are co-chaired by the World Bank vice president for South Asia and the Bangladesh finance minister. The government wrote a letter to the World Bank in that it wanted the finance minister of Bangladesh to chair the BDF meeting.[7]

The BNP led government was of the view that member countries were able to raise uncomfortable questions because the World Bank has been setting the agenda of the BDF meetings in consultation with the donors. It also hoped that by taking charge it would be able to dominate the agenda-setting meets. Though the move would not have completely silenced the donors it would have definitely reduced the scope for the donors to speak up at an appropriate platform.

Donor Funding, an Important part of Bangladesh Budget Making

The importance of foreign donations for budget making in Bangladesh was soon realised by Saifur Rahman. While addressing the Economic Reporters Forum (ERF) in Dhaka on 16 March 2005 he confessed that the country's foreign currency reserves were under acute pressure because of higher imports. He hoped to maintain the reserve with the "development support from the donors."

At that time Bangladesh has also not been doing well on the export front because its main export—readymade garments was impacted by the post-MFA regime. The country felt the sting of the quota-phase out just one month after it was passed in January 2005, with export earnings plummeting at an alarming rate and indicating a bleak performance in the coming months.

Around this time, Bangladesh also had the opportunity of becoming part of the MCA programme. To take advantages of this programme, Bangladesh tried to project itself as a moderate Muslim majority democracy. The Bangladesh police prevented nearly 3000 Islamic activists of the radical Islamic Constitution Movement (ICM) from laying siege to the US embassy. They were demonstrating against the reported desecration of the Quran by US troops at the Guantanamo Bay detention centre in Cuba. The protesters carrying banners and placards chanted slogans against Bush, Blair and the Israeli prime minister Ariel Sharon, calling them enemies of Islam. They also accused them of persecuting Muslims in Iraq and the Palestinian territories. The ICM secretary general Moulana Mohammad Hemayetuddin said: "The insult on (sic) the holy Koran can not be tolerated. Bush and Blair must apologise, otherwise the flame of anger will continue to hunt them everywhere."

Calculated Crackdown on Islamist Terror

The four-party alliance government in Bangladesh would make a token crackdown on Islamists whenever international pressure intensified. It would also tighten noose on the extremists before a donor meet. The government also had to face elections towards the end of 2006 and to give these elections some kind of credibility in the face of strong demands by the opposition for electoral reform, Bangladesh government resorted to a crackdown. Previously the government had chosen to dismiss Islamist terror in Bangladesh as a 'media creation' and a 'foreign worry'.[8]

As a result, Sheikh Abdur Rahman, chief of the banned Jama'atul Mujaheedin Bangladesh (JMB), who terrorised Bangladesh with his ruthless squad of bombers and preferred death to surrender in the cause of jihad, surrendered meekly before the Rapid Action Battalion (RAB) on 2 March 2006 at a house in the northeastern city of Sylhet.[9] He was arrested along with his two other accomplices. His deputy, Bangla Bhai, who headed the JMJB, was arrested in Mymensingh on 6 March 2006. The ease with which the law enforcement agencies arrested them showed that the government could have done so earlier if it had so desired.

The bomb expert of JMB, Shakil alias Mollah Omar was killed in an encounter by RAB on 13 March 2006 in Comilla while they were searching for Mohammad Salahuddin, another key member of JMB, and a close associate of Abdur Rahman. Along with Shakil three of his family members were also killed in bomb explosions carried out by them to resist the raid. The RAB during this raid also arrested JMB supremo Abdur Rahman's son Nabil Rahman along with a JMB cadre Alamgir alias Bijoy alias Shaikat.

The JMB started calling Shakil, Mollah Omar, as he proved his expertise in bomb making. It was Shakil who supplied the explosives that were used for killing two judges in Jhalakathi on 14 November 2005. This was disclosed by Hasan Al Mamun the suicide bomber who killed the two judges—Jagannath Pandey and Sohel Ahmed—before his death.

Half-hearted Crackdown Increases Problems for the BNP Government

The arrest of some Islamist militants by the BNP government was cautiously welcomed by several quarters because it also raised the possibility of retaliation by these outfits whose network and striking capability was still intact. The United States indefinitely suspended the activities of the Peace Corps fearing possible attacks in retaliation for the capture of militant leaders. The US decision irked the Bangladeshi government with the foreign minister, M. Morshed Khan, and the state minister for home affairs Lutfozzaman Babar, criticising the decision saying that there was no reason for it. The same was reiterated by the foreign secretary, Hemayet Uddin, who said that the withdrawal by the Peace Corps is "an ill-advised decision and there is no reason to do it."[10] The U.S. Embassy also agreed with Bangladesh government's sentiment but at the same time, US Diplomatic Charge d' Affaires in Bangladesh, Judith A. Chammas, said that the decision to suspend US Peace Corps activities in Bangladesh was based on "credible but not unsubstantiated threat against the Peace Corps volunteers."[11]

The US also feared that the limited action against the Islamist militants might encourage them to target the establishments of the US and other Western countries. As a result it issued a travel alert to its citizens. The announcement said, "It remains unclear whether JMB, despite its recent setbacks, retains the ability to launch new attacks. The target of new JMB attacks could be Americans, other Westerners or Bangladeshis."[12] The US embassy advised its citizens extra care and precaution while going out in public, especially if visiting courts or municipal government offices.

Though the official stand of the Bangladesh government was different, its ministers too feared that the Islamist might retaliate. On 23 March 2006 Lutfozzaman Babar, reportedly said, "We are not ruling out the possibility of further attacks by the Islamic militants despite their top leaders were arrested early this month." He also stated that his ministry has asked the security forces to remain alert. Confirming his apprehension the outlawed JMB on 30 March 2006 threatened to kill a district court judge in Dinajpur with his family and blow up the court if he failed to release JMB activists. The threat was reportedly made in a letter sent to Additional District Judge Md Zahedur Rahman.

Conviction of Islamists

It appeared that the government was keen to rein in Islamists before the upcoming elections, but this could not be accomplished just by arresting a few top leaders. At this point, it asked the judiciary to take follow up action. Taking their cue from the government, Bangladesh courts in series of judgements, passed in the first half of 2006 convicted Islamist extremists in cases pertaining to bombing and explosions at public places.[13] This was a surprising development in a country where Islamic parties were part of the ruling coalition and the government so known for its soft attitude towards them. Unfortunately these actions by government failed to diminish the strength of Islamic groups.

- A court in Feni on 3 July 2006 sentenced six JMB members for life for the 17 August bombings in the district.
- A court in Kurigram on 18 July 2006 awarded life imprisonment to four activists of JMB for their involvement in serial blasts in the district town on 17 August 2006.
- A court in Laxmipur sentenced three JMB members—Ataur Rahman Sunny, Masumur Rahman and Amzad Ali—to death in connection with 2005 bombings on 15 August 2006.[14] Five others were given life terms for their alleged roles in the bombings. Ataur Rahman Sunny had already been sentenced to death, along with JMB Chief Abdur Rahman and another JMB leader Siddiqul Islam—alias Bangla Bhai, for killing two judges in 2005.

- The Bangladesh High Court (HC) on 31 August confirmed the death sentences for seven militant leaders of the JMB including its five kingpins for killing two judges in Jhalakathi as it found the trial court's judgment appropriate.
- Eight JMB militants were sentenced to life imprisonment in separate cases in Thakurgaon and Rajshahi on 31 August 2006.
- Three cadres of JMB were sentenced to 12 years' rigorous imprisonment by a special tribunal in Jamalpur on 17 September 2006 for possessing explosives and bomb making materials.[15]

Convictions Fail to Break Terror Network

Unfortunately, these convictions failed to break the terror network in Bangladesh. Towards the end of July 2006 the government alerted law enforcement and intelligence agencies to step up vigilance across the country following information that JMB militants were reorganising themselves under different banners. Reports also indicated that the militants were trying to regroup in the haor and beel areas of the north and north-eastern region after a decline in their activities due to arrest of most of their top leaders. This attempt to revive their activities was made by the lower rung leaders who were still outside the security dragnet.

These reports were proven true when on 2 August 2006 the RAB captured 26 Islamist militants while training in a remote jungle in Mymensingh. The captured militants included two prospective suicide bombers and a veteran of the Afghan war. The RAB confirmed that the militants belonged to the JMB. Sheikh Hasina who was in the opposition at that time termed these arrests as nothing but eyewash to please the visiting US assistant secretary of state.

Arrests of JMB Leaders to Pacify Western Countries

The arrest of JMB leaders failed to produce the desired result because the government was not serious about acting against the terror groups operating within the country. The Awami League and its front organisations termed the arrest a "drama" by the government to impress the world community ahead of the elections. The party also felt that the arrests came at a time when the government was facing flak for the acute crises in the power, fuel and fertiliser sectors.

The government tried to extract maximum mileage from the arrest of Sheikh Abdur Rahman. On the day of the arrest Prime Minister Khaleda Zia in an address to nation over radio and television said that Bangladesh has proved to the world community that it could successfully combat terrorism in the name of Islam. The prime minister "thanked the friendly countries who extended their cooperation in the form of advice, training, technical and technological assistance, particularly Interpol, FBI and the Scotland Yard, in combating the militancy."[16]

By these arrests, the Bangladesh government probably wanted to pacify western countries. In this effort they were somewhat successful. The capture of Sheikh Abdur Rahman was welcomed by the United States, the United Kingdom and the European Union. A US embassy spokesman reportedly said, "We welcome the capture of Abdur Rahman as a significant step forward in the government's response to the JMB's campaign of terror."[17] The US government also felt that the arrest would prove to be a blow to extremists who want to create an Islamic state in the country. The US state department spokesman Adam Ereli also termed it as a sign of the successful cooperation between the US and Bangladesh in the fight against terror.

Through these actions though the BNP led government managed to pacify the Western countries it failed to produce impact on militant organisations. The militant outfits had often close links with the BNP and Jamaat leaders whose political patronage did not allow the law enforcement agencies to take any effective action against them.

Symbiotic Relationship

There was a symbiotic relationship between the BNP, the Jamaat and the militant outfits who were being used by the BNP and Jamaat against their political adversaries. This was seen very clearly during the trial of several cases. The BNP and Jamaat leaders managed to influence the outcome of the trial of the 1999 Jessore Udichi bombing. All the 23 accused went scot-free owing to lack of evidence against them. In fact the working of the investigating agencies in Bangladesh forced the honourable judge to comment that the shoddy work done by them has prevented the real perpetrators from being brought to justice. As the Udichi case straddled two regimes, it gave the police ample opportunity to botch up the evidence when the regime changed after 2001 elections. Several US lawmakers also expressed their concern about the Kibria case (Former Finance Minister SAMS Kibria was killed in a public meeting on 17 January 2005) going nowhere.

Authorities Tried To Delay Trial of JMB Men

The trials of several cases filed against leaders and activists of the outlawed JMB were delayed as the authorities concerned were reluctant to produce the charge-sheeted accused before the courts in Dhaka. Courts concerned could not frame charges against the detained militants or start trials of at least a dozen cases as the jail authorities and law enforcement agencies did not produce the JMB leaders and activists before the court on the scheduled dates. In some cases accused militants were not produced before the courts for more than ten consecutive dates. The courts repeatedly directed the jail authorities and law enforcement agencies to produce the accused, but the orders were ignored.

JMB Leaders Provided Special Treatment

The four-party alliance government provided special treatment to the jailed JMB leaders. Both Abdur Rahman and Siddiqul Islam Banglabhai were kept in a 'special jail' in Mirpur instead of secured cells of a prison. Jail authorities claimed that the two top militant leaders were kept in a house in a residential area "isolated from people" to ensure "special security." On the other hand, the four-party alliance government chose to keep the killers of Bangabandhu Sheikh Mujibur Rahman in the Dhaka Central Jail.

Hanging of Condemned Militants Postponed

JMB militants had killed senior assistant judges Jagannath Pandey and Sohel Ahmed in a suicide bomb attack at Purba Chadkati in Jhalakathi town on 14 November 2005. For this crime seven militants—Rahman, Bangla Bhai, Sunny, Awal, Khaled Saifullah, Mamun and Asadul Islam alias Arif—were condemned to death on 29 May 2006 by Reza Tarik Ahmed, the Additional District and Sessions Judge of Jhalakathi. The High Court confirmed the death sentences on 31 August.

All the JMB leaders, after their capture, repeatedly said on different occasions that they would not accept trial and verdict under Taguti (non-Islamic) laws and by any worldly court. They also said on several occasions that they would not appeal against the death penalties.

Abdur Rahman and Bangla Bhai repeated in a letter through jail authorities that it was justified to kill people in the cause of establishing Islamic rule and that the judges, who had tried them, deserved death. In this letter though Rahman and Bangla Bhai did not seek to appeal against death penalty, the Supreme Court (SC) registrar ordered on 1 October to stay their executions considering their letters as prayer for appeal.

Other militants who had been condemned to death for killing judges were also not executed. They had sought permission to appeal against their sentences after the due date. The Supreme Court registrar on 3 October 2006 stayed the execution of the death penalty of Ata-ur-Rahman Sunny and the Majlish-e-Shura member Abdul Awal, following their special prayer through the jail authorities for leave to appeal. Sunny and Awal submitted their prayers to the Dhaka Central Jail authorities on 2 October, three days after the time limit for appeal had expired. The SC registrar sent separate letters to the home ministry, jail and the other authorities concerned, ordering postponement of the execution.

Terror Remained a Point of Contention with India During BNP Regime

After India completed the fencing along its western border with Pakistan, there has been a corresponding rise in the infiltration of Islamist militants over the Bangladesh border. The terror attacks in which the terrorists either came from Bangladesh or through that country has been a matter of concern for India. The role of HuJI was suspected in several serial blasts that took place in India. This Indian concern was conveyed to Bangladesh on the eve of the Khaleda Zia's visit to India.

But Bangladesh remained reluctant to act against extremists. The country insisted that it did not harbour terrorists, and its ties with India could not improve as long as this 'erroneous impression' persisted. On the last day of a three-day visit to India by Prime Minister Khaleda Zia, the Bangladesh finance minister M Saifur Rahman said, "This is an erroneous impression. As long as this erroneous impression remains, relations between India and Bangladesh cannot improve."[18] He said Bangladesh was shocked to hear that some of its nationals were involved in the terror attacks in Varanasi and other places.

Lack of Direction During the Fakharuddin Ahmed led Caretaker Government

The caretaker government headed by Fakharuddin Ahmed remained in power from 13 January 2007 to 29 December 2008. It attempted to bring about many changes in the polity of Bangladesh. It devoted large part of its time on trying to introduce political reforms and anti-corruption. Interestingly, these demands were raised by Sheikh Hasina herself. However, the way caretaker government chose to do that, it created difficulty for both Hasina and Khaleda. In fact, the caretaker government mooted the policy of minus-two formula under which it wanted to banish leaders of both the mainstream political parties from their political life. But the caretaker government failed in its endeavour as it could not evolve any alternative political force. Their attempt to create a third political force under the leadership of Mohamed Yunus failed to take off.

This approach created suspicion in the minds of many people who were concerned as the caretaker government had not taken any similar action against the leaders of Jamaat-e-Islami. Though the caretaker government had executed six top leaders of the JMB it was difficult to fully understand the motive behind it.

No doubt, executing Islamist leaders in a Muslim majority country was no mean achievement it was done on the eve of the Delhi SAARC summit. It was possible that this step was taken to get some kind of acceptability for the government in Dhaka which was in a sense unconstitutional as caretaker governments according to the constitution of Bangladesh were supposed to be in power for only 90 days during which they have to hold elections and transfer power to an elected government. It was also said that the top leaders of the JMB were hurriedly executed because like Mufti Hannan they also wanted to talk to media which could have created problems for their patrons in Bangladesh.

The caretaker government in Bangladesh had claimed that it had assumed power with the objective of bringing about a new political culture in the country. This aim had made them decide upon a crackdown against corruption and the introduction of a slew of political reforms. One such reform was the need for all parties to abide by the constitution and non-registration of religion based parties. But when Bangladesh appeared to be heading towards parliamentary elections, the military-backed caretaker government sprung a surprise by allowing the registration of a terrorist group, Harkat-ul-Jihad-e-Islami (HuJI), as a political party. This step of the Bangladesh Election Commission raised questions about the sincerity of ongoing political reforms. For a while, it appeared that the caretaker government was unwilling to take any serious action against HuJI militants because it wanted to legitimize their activities. Thus despite several steps taken in favour of political reforms and anti-corruption the caretaker government failed to provide any clear-cut direction on counter-terrorism.

Crackdown on Terror During the Awami League Government

The actual crackdown on terror started during the second term of the Sheikh Hasina government for which there were several reasons:

Attacks on Awami League Leaders

Attacks on Awami League leaders had begun even during the first term of

Sheikh Hasina's government including the attempt on the life of Hasina herself in Kotalipara, Gopalganj in 2000.[19] Mufti Mohammad Hannan, operations commander of HuJI was the prime accused in this case.

Subsequently, during the BNP led government a large number of Awami League leaders were attacked and many of them were killed. Seven major terror attacks took place between May 2004 and December 2005 in which 34 people were killed and over 400 were injured.

In a gruesome attack on a Sheikh Hasina rally in Dhaka on 21 August 2004, 24 Awami League leaders and workers were killed and over 200 injured. Sheikh Hasina too barely survived. But a senior party leader Ivy Rahman, the wife of President Zillur Rahman, was killed and Hasina nearly became deaf.

Five people were killed and 70 injured in the attack on finance minster SAMS Kibria. In the attack on Suranjit Sengupta one person was killed and over 30 were injured. Similarly one person was killed and over 30 were injured in the attack that took place on the Sylhet mayor. In the attack on Syeda Jebunnessa Haque at least eight persons were injured.[20] The terrorists also targeted the Bangladesh-born British high commissioner at the shrine of Hazrat Shahjalal. In this attack three persons were killed and 70 injured.

These attacks were mostly carried out by the Islamists for whom the Awami League was the enemy and an obstacle in the path of an Islamic state. They also considered the party to be anti-Islam and pro-India. Anwar Choudhury was targeted, as he too was considered to be an enemy by HuJI.

The Islamic militants in Bangladesh especially HuJI started using Arges grenades in 2004. Earlier, they were using locally-made bombs. These grenades used in the attack on Sheikh Hasina in 2004 were sent to HuJI - Bangladesh by the Pakistan-based militant LeT. These facts did not come to light during the BNP-Jamaat alliance rule or even during the two-year rule of the caretaker government as investigations were not conducted properly. The probes were politicised during the BNP-Jamaat rule. Some of those did not progress for dillydallying tactics, while others were diverted to save the real culprits.

However, Mufti Mohammad Hannan, operations commander of HuJI was arrested on 1 October 2005 after the countrywide bomb blasts. Hannan and two of his accomplices in 2007 confessed before a magistrate that they carried out the 2004 grenade attack targeting Sheikh Hasina following a High Court ban on religious fatwas and for the action against leaders and workers of the Islamist organisations.[21]

Several HuJI men were convicted in the Anwar Choudhury attack case. Mufti Abdul Hannan, Sharif Shahedul, Alam Bipul and Delwar Hossain alias Ripon were sentenced to death, while Hannan's brother, Muhibullah alias Muhibur Rahman alias Ovi, and Mufti Main Uddin alias Abu Zandal were awarded life imprisonment. The law enforcement agencies say that Hannan, Bipul, Ovi and Zandal were involved in the murder of Kibria.

It is very clear that Islamic militants were involved in the killing of Awami League leaders. The way one after the other senior Awami League leaders were being wiped out, it became clear that if the party has to remain politically relevant, they need to check such elements for whom even killing political opponents is not unthinkable.

Terror Tears Apart Pakistan

In Bangladesh there is a section which is apologetic of the Liberation War. Islamists are most important part of this section. But there are also people who are fence-sitters. These people believe in centre right political parties, but they may not be willing to adopt the terror tactics used by the Islamists. However, when Islamist groups whom Pakistan so assiduously cultivated as strategic asset started creating problem for the country then barring extremists all other sections in country started rethinking about Pakistan being a role model for the country.

This was also the period when a fast-paced economic growth was taking place in India. India showed the prospect of emerging as a major global power. However, it is also true that the rightist elements were also fearful of India's growth and its emergence as a major power. But the economic growth of India and turmoil in Pakistan made them decide that latter was not a suitable model for Bangladesh. Hence the party representing that model was not desirable. In the 2008 elections a major part of these fence sitters voted for the Awami League and brought it to power.

Resurgence of the Spirit of the Liberation War

During the run-up to the 2008 elections there was a massive resurgence of the spirit of the Liberation War. In this a major role was played by the freedom fighters of Bangladesh. Sector Commander Maj Gen (retd) KM Shafiullah requested the people, "not to let any war criminals go to parliament as we have got our parliament in exchange of three million lives."[22] They also ran a campaign against all the war criminals contesting the polls, especially the Jamaat Amir Motiur Rahman Nizami, supreme commander of Al Badr Bahini, secretary general Ali Ahsan Mohammad Mojaheed, head of the Al Badr in

Dhaka, and alleged war criminals Delwar Hossain Sayeedi and Salahuddin Qader Chowdhury.

Sammilito Sangskritik Jote, a group of civil society organisations, too vowed to boycott war criminals in the national elections. A call for not voting in favour of war criminals and communal forces was also given by 'Bikkhubdha Deshbasi.' The activities of freedom fighters on the eve of elections moblised people in favour of pro-liberation forces. They created awareness among the younger generation about the sacrifices made and the atrocities committed by the extremist elements on their own people. In this election a large number of people were those who had voted for the first time and their awareness about liberation helped a pro-liberation party come to power.

Jamaat, a key component of the four party combine, however tried to weaken the movement of freedom fighters through propaganda and by misleading people.[23] It floated a fake freedom fighter body. In its election manifesto it offered to strengthen the liberation war ministry and the Freedom Fighters Welfare Trust and increase allowances for the freedom fighters' families. This was an attempt to win over the freedom fighters. Fortunately, people saw through their designs and defeated them in the elections. BNP and Jamaat once again tried to get votes in name of Islam but were not very successful in their effort.

Awami League, however, this time was clearly against the militants. The Awami League president Sheikh Hasina pledged to take measures to stop repression on religious minorities and build a Bangladesh free from poverty and hunger, if voted to power.[24]

Action Against Terror Groups under Awami League

The coming to power of Sheikh Hasina for the second time was a major development in the democratic history of Bangladesh. Now it was clear to the Awami League leaders that if the party had to survive then it had to be clear about its political philosophy. This was reiterated by Sheikh Hasina in her very first press conference after winning the elections when she declared that she will not allow the country's soil to be used by terror groups and proposed a joint South Asia task force in the subcontinent to tackle terror.[25]

South Asia Task-Force

Counter-terrorism and elimination of religious extremism had figured prominently in the election manifesto of Sheikh Hasina. To fulfil this promise she proposed that a South Asia task force be constituted with the objective to track down militants and bring them to justice as well as to strengthen cooperation between the police forces and judiciaries of South Asian nations.[26]

However, Hasina's proposal faced strong domestic resistance. The main opposition BNP was of the opinion that countries like Pakistan would be unenthusiastic about it. The party launched a blistering attack against the proposal when Sheikh Hasina discussed the proposal with Indian foreign minister Pranab Mukherjee. They thought that the proposed South Asia task force was a euphemism for signing a bilateral agreement with India that would allow Indian forces into Bangladesh. BNP Secretary General Khandaker Delwar Hossain threatened that a bilateral mechanism of this type would turn Bangladesh into a "Gaza". He also feared that it might lead to insurgent activities from India's Northeast spilling over to Bangladesh. Hossain also said:

We firmly believe that our people, conventional laws, law enforcing agencies and the armed forces are capable enough to keep the country free from militancy and strife. Signing any deal with other countries outside international conventions to contain militancy is unnecessary and could prove suicidal.[27]

The Jamaat also warned the Hasina government of trouble if it went ahead with its plan. The party chief Matiur Rahman Nizami felt that the Bangladesh police, BDR, RAB and army had enough capacity to curb terrorism in the country. He also warned against inviting foreign troops into the country and criticised the government for its impatience to sign "anti-people" agreements like the regional anti-terrorism task force, transit facilities for India and the Trade and Investment Framework Agreement (TIFA) with the United States.[28]

It's quite clear that the opposition parties tried to mislead people into thinking that it was a ploy to bring Indian forces inside Bangladesh. They also feared that any meaningful counter-terror cooperation would dismantle what the BNP and Jamaat had been trying to put in place over the years.

In addition to domestic resistance, the regional task force proposal also has to contend with the realities of the divergent interests of South Asian countries. There is little doubt that cooperation is necessary to combat terrorism in South Asia, and it was with this objective that South Asian countries had adopted the SAARC Convention on Terrorism in 1987. At the 11th Summit in Kathmandu in January 2002, leaders of SAARC had taken a pledge to make collective efforts to stamp out terrorism. The SAARC convention on terrorism was reinforced by the adoption of an Additional Protocol on terrorism at the 12th Summit whose modalities were finalised in the Dhaka Summit. The SAARC established a Terrorist Offences Monitoring Desk (STOMD) in Colombo to collate, analyse and disseminate information about terrorist incidents, tactics, strategies and methods. But for regional efforts to bear fruit, all member states have to show equal commitment. This has however not been the case. Hasina subsequently realised this and called for good relations between Pakistan and India.

BDR Mutiny Delays Action Against Terror

The Sheikh Hasina government however could not immediately take action against the terrorists and insurgents because there was a major mutiny in the para-military Bangladesh Rifles (BDR) only two months after assuming office. This mutiny threatened to create political instability in Bangladesh which was avoided due to the tactful handling of the situation. Though three enquiry committees were set up to probe the incident, not much information was available about the causes of mutiny which was suspected to have been organised by the extremist elements at the instance of a foreign power.[29] The government managed to avert a political crisis, but it delayed action against terror.

Reorganisation of Counter-Terrorism Structure

The BDR mutiny might have delayed action against terrorism but it also brought to the notice of the government that the security and counter-terror structure in the country needed to be reorganised. The government had begun the process of change even before the mutiny took place by appointing a new director of the DGFI. This was necessitated by the continuing bad publicity received by the Directorate General of Forces Intelligence (DGFI). The change was done under an army shuffle involving several two-star generals.

Mollah Fazle Akbar, who joined the army in 1976, was promoted to major general and made the new head of the DGFI.[30] Akbar succeeded Maj Gen Golam Mohammad, who moved to Comilla to head the 33 Infantry Division. Maj Gen Abul Kalam was asked to take charge of the Infantry Division based in Rangpur. Brig Gen Mahbub Haider Khan was made new military secretary.

There was a major shake-up in the security apparatus after the bloody mutiny in Bangladesh Rifles (BDR). The government also ordered the beefing up of security at key installations across Bangladesh after a home ministry report indicated that some of the nearly a dozen militant outfits active in the country may have a hand in the February revolt in the BDR. Brigadier-

General (retd) Manzur Ahmed was appointed as the new Director General of NSI, the country's main intelligence agency, replacing Major General Sheikh Monirul Islam.[31] The change of guard in the spy agency came in the wake of the reports alleging intelligence failure in getting inputs on the BDR mutiny which left at least 73 army officers dead. The government also named new heads of the CID, the special branch of the police and a new chief of Military Intelligence.

Two-Pronged Action

The Sheikh Hasina government has adopted a two-pronged approach against terror groups. It has acted against domestic Islamist groups like HuJI, and JMB. Action against them has exposed their international links. Now it has been decisively proved that these groups have been acting in concert with international terrorist outfits like the LeT, Hizbul Mujahideen and the JeM. Though groups like LeT, JeM are headquartered in Pakistan they have modules in Bangladesh. The government also banned many of the activities of the Hizb-ut-Tahrir (Party of Liberation) and declared it antistate, anti-government, anti-people, and anti-democracy.[32]

More importantly, Sheikh Hasina's government has also acted against Indian insurgent groups which have so far successfully used the territory of Bangladesh to conduct terror activities inside India.[33] In her earlier tenure, Sheikh Hasina could not act decisively against these groups. But it seems that Hasina's landslide victory and terror attacks directed at her during the previous four-party coalition rule has made her more resolute in acting against terror.

Action Against Domestic Islamist Groups

As the Sheikh Hasina government was determined to act against the domestic Islamist terror groups it gave clear instructions to the law enforcement agencies to go after these groups. This allowed them to bust a number of modules of local Islamist groups like JMB and HuJI.

A large number of LeT operatives were arrested from Bangladesh and from India on the basis of information provided by David Headley and Tahawwur Rana. These arrests not only helped avert another 26/11 kind of attack against Indian and the US interests in Bangladesh, but also brought to fore the extensive LeT networks in the sub-continent.

David Coleman Headley, also known as Dawood Sayed Gilani, a Pakistan-origin US national, was arrested in the United States in October 2009 by the Federal Bureau of Investigation's Joint Terrorism Task Force at

O'Hare International Airport while en route to Pakistan. He was held for plotting terror attacks on behalf of the LeT against India and on charges of plotting a terror attack against the facilities and employees of the Danish newspaper which had published cartoons of the Prophet Mohammed in 2005. Tahawwur Hussain Rana is a Canadian citizen of Pakistani origin. Alleged to be Headley's accomplice, he has also been named in the case of the now foiled terror attacks plotted by the LeT. Subsequently, another Pakistani national, Abdur Rahman Sayeed, linked to LeT, was arrested in Pakistan in the first week of November.

The three had ordered LeT men in Bangladesh to attack the US and Indian embassies. On the basis of leads provided by US agencies, detectives in Bangladesh foiled the plot. In the process they arrested Mufti Harun Izahar and his two associates from a madrassa in Chittagong. Mufti Harun Izahar is the son of IOJ leader Mufti Izaharul Islam Chowdhury.[34] Harun had been in regular contact with the two LeT operatives detained in the United States and the one held in Pakistan.

Harun's cellphone call list revealed that a Pakistani national by the name of Azmol was leading Pakistani LeT terrorists in Bangladesh. However he along with two other Pakistani militants managed to flee Bangladesh. But police arrested three other Pakistani nationals—Mohammad Monwar, Mohammad Ashraf Ali Zahid and Syed Abdul Kaiyum alias Sufian—linked with LeT.

Bangladesh police later arrested another local LeT operative, a Bangladeshi national Abu Motaleb alias Matu alias Majnu, from Dhaka.[35] Motaleb is an Afghan war veteran and was in charge of co-ordinating the foiled attacks on the US and Indian missions. He has also been in close contact with both HuJI and LeT. He had participated in a meeting that was held in Rajshahi before the terror attacks were carried out in the Indian cities of Hyderabad and Bangalore.

There were two Indians—T. Nasir and Sharfaraz of Kerala in the 15-member LeT commando squad tasked to attack the US and Indian missions in Dhaka on 26 November 2009. Both of them were arrested by the Indian police on 6 November 2009 soon after they crossed the Bibir Bazar border in Comilla, possibly on the basis of information provided by the Bangladesh police.[36] The two LeT operatives were earlier hiding in the hilly areas of Chittagong for around one and a half months and trying to collect explosives from the Rohingya rebels for the attack. Funds for launching the attacks on the US Embassy and Indian High Commission were reportedly provided by LeT leaders in Pakistan.

The increased pressure of Bangladesh police forced present chief (Amir) of Jama'atul Mujaheedin Bangladesh (JMB), Maulana Saidur Rahman to sneak into India. Rahman and his son Abu Talha Muhammad Fahim alias Bashar narrowly escaped a Rapid Action Battalion (RAB) raid on a hideout in Sabujganj near Dhaka on 1 November 2009. However, in this raid, his wife and a couple of others were arrested.[37] The documents and SIM cards seized by RAB officials exposed his network across Bangladesh and his links with Indian northeast insurgent outfits. JMB is believed to be the mentor of Indian Northeast insurgents and Islamist terror masterminds who have been in Bangladesh for years.

It is believed that Rahman played a crucial role in jihadist activities in Bangladesh and that his organisation worked in tandem with the Bangladesh chapters of LeT and HuJI which have been responsible for several terror attacks in India. On the instructions of their Pakistani handlers, Rahman and his brigade arranged for the training and shelter of LeT and HuJI operatives. Most Indian Northeast militant leaders, including the top rung of ULFA, were allegedly under Rahman's protection, and the cadres were trained by the JMB.[38]

The Bangladesh police have also busted a Jaish-e-Mohammed (JeM) module. The arrests were made by the Rapid Action Battalion (RAB) of Bangladesh from Dhaka on 28 February 2010. Out of the five arrested persons one was a Pakistani national while the other four were his local associates. According to security officials in Bangladesh, the Pakistani, Rezwan Ahmed, had been coordinating JeM operations in the country. He was recruiting locals for the terror outfit and sending them for training in Pakistan. The trained extremists were then used for launching terror attacks in India. Ahmed was freely moving between India and Bangladesh. The four arrested Bangladeshis were—Nannu Mian alias Belal Mandol alias Billal, Abu Naser Munshi, Imad Uddin alias Munna, and Sadeque Hossain alias Khoka. In this operation the RAB also recovered the passport of another Pakistani named Jawad who managed to flee to India.

Rezwan revealed to his interrogators that he had been trained to operate AK-47, machine guns, sniper rifles, rocket-propelled grenades and explosive devices. But the most startling disclosure was made by Nannu Mian alias Belal Mandol alias Billal, who claimed that he had a role in hijacking the Indian Airlines plane in late December 1999. He had served ten years in Guwahati jail, though on a different charge. After release from prison, he fled to Bangladesh and was plotting new terror strikes against India when he was caught. In India, security agencies however are still not sure about the involvement of Billal in the IC 814 hijacking.

These Jaish terrorists were arrested from Sukanya Tower in Dhaka. They were sheltered by Mohiuddin and his brother Salahuddin who were residing in Sukanya Tower. Mohiuddin, who is presently president of Hajiganj union Bangladesh Nationalist Party (BNP) in Chandpur, had earlier been involved in the activities of Jamaat-e-Islami. Both Mohiuddin and Salahuddin have also visited Pakistan.

Though these arrests have given a setback to Pakistani terror modules, it has also raised concerns about the actual scale of the operations of Pakistan-based terrorist groups in that country. Many in Bangladesh argue that the country has unwittingly become host to such groups but these extremists cannot be shelterd in Bangladesh unless there is a section which subscribes to similar radical ideology. This indicates that there is a constituency in Bangladesh which supports such elements. These extremists would create a much bigger problem for the whole region, if they get state support, as was the case during the four-party coalition rule. Unless there is a consensus across political spectrum to act against these terror groups, the present action would only mean a temporary breather for India.

War Crime Trial

The prosecution of war criminals is another major step taken by the Sheikh Hasina government. During the liberation war, the Jamaat was enlisted by the Pakistani army to act against Bangladeshi freedom fighters. Jamaat which wanted united Pakistan committed atrocities on people who were fighting to over throw the oppressive West Pakistani rule. Certain other right wing leaders were also engaged in these acts. After Ghulam Azam escaped from Bangladesh on 22 November 1971, he formed "East Pakistan Restoration Committee" in Lahore. He used the committee to launch an anti-Bangladesh movement in the name of an Islamic movement and tried to influence the Middle East into not recognising Bangladesh.[39] Since these people escaped lightly after the liberation, they managed to revive their extremist and anti-democratic politics.

In the run-up to the election Sheikh Hasina had promised that her government would take action against these war criminals. The International Crimes Tribunal is trying the former Jamaat Amir Ghulam Azam, the present Amir Motiur Rahman Nizami, Muhammad Kamaruzzaman, Delawar Hossain Sayedee and some other prominent Jamaat leaders. The BNP leader Salauddin Quader Chowdhury is also being tried.

Ghulam Azam considered by many as the symbol of war crimes during the Liberation War of Bangladesh, has now been indicted on five charges of crimes against humanity. The charges against Ghulam Azam include involvement in murder and torture of unarmed people; and conspiracy, planning, incitement and complicity to commit genocide and crimes against humanity during the 1971 war.[40] The tribunal has also indicted Matiur Rahman Nizami on 16 charges, including murder and genocide and Abdul Quader Molla, a deputy of Nizami, for his alleged involvement in crimes against humanity.[41] The government thinks that the important part of the war crime trial would be over by the end of 2012.[42]

The government is taking this step in spite of grave risk to its survival. The BNP and Jamaat are trying various tactics to scuttle the trials. In fact, the BDR mutiny and the army coup are also seen as part of this strategy. But the government seems determined to conduct this trial and take it to its logical conclusion. Prime Minister Sheikh Hasina has urged the Sector Commanders' Forum (SCF) to mobilise public opinion against the "opposition's move" to protect the war criminals.[43] If the trials are successful and the process is taken to its logical conclusion then it is expected that it will further contain radicalism in Bangladeshi society.

Crackdown Against Northeast Insurgents

For a long time, India has been accusing Bangladesh of sheltering Northeast insurgents and not acting against them. This complaint has been addressed significantly during the present regime of Sheikh Hasina. The crackdown started with action against ULFA. In the first week of November 2009, self-styled foreign secretary of ULFA Sashadhar Choudhury and finance secretary Chitraban Hazarika were handed over to Indian security forces. But the most important action was the decision to hand over Arabinda Rajkhowa, Chairman of ULFA who is now in the custody of the Assam Police along with his bodyguard Palash Phukan alias Raja Bora and Deputy Commander-in-Chief Hitesh Kalita alias Raju Barua.[44] Subsequently, Bangladesh pushed out three other top leaders of the outfit across the India-Bangladesh border at Dawki in Meghalaya. They were ULFA "captain" Antu Chaudang, "second lieutenant" Pradeep Chetia and another cadre called Saurav. Chaudang was once a close associate of "commander-in-chief" Paresh Baruah.[45]

This development was also significant as there is no bilateral extradition treaty between India and Bangladesh. However, as the Hasina government was determined to cooperate on countering terror it did not allow the absence of extradition treaty to be a handicap. To overcome this hurdle New Delhi and Dhaka reached a tacit understanding that Northeast rebels based in Bangladesh will be simply picked up and handed over to India.[46]

Most ULFA leaders had taken up Muslim aliases. At the time of their "detention," Hazarika was living under the name of Ashfaqul Hossein, while Choudhury was known as Rafiqul Islam. They also had Bangladeshi voter identity cards and passports. Bangladeshi intelligence sleuths had seized these documents from Choudhary and Hazarika before handing them over to India.

The handover of the top brass of ULFA, except for Paresh Barua who appears not to be in Bangladesh at present, gave a big jolt to the outfit. Though it is true that in recent times ULFA has been singlehandedly managed by Paresh Barua and other leaders like Rajkhowa have played only a marginal role, their arrest will be a major setback for the outfit. Rajkhowa is not only chairman of ULFA but also its main ideologue and founding member. His arrest is bound to dampen the spirit of Paresh Barua who is now bereft of his former comrades.

Action has also been taken against other insurgent groups and many of their training camps have been destroyed. However, some of the other top insurgent leaders like Biswamohan Debbarma of the National Liberation Front of Tripura (NLFT) and Ranjit Debbarma of the All Tripura Tiger Force (ATTF) are still suspected to be hiding in Bangladesh. India is also trying extradition of ULFA leader Anup Chetia.

The action against the Indian insurgent groups also improved the internal security of Bangladesh. In October 2009, Home Minister Shamsul Haque Tuku stated that the law enforcement agencies were asked to crack down on ULFA bases following intelligence reports that the group was planning major strikes in Dhaka. It was feared that as the comfort level of Indian insurgent outfits based in Dhaka dipped, they would indulge in some terror activity even inside Bangladesh. In this context, the crackdown against ULFA and the handover of their leaders, despite the absence of a formal extradition mechanism, helped to improve the internal security situation of both countries.

Notes

1. Inam Ahmed, "Washington Meet: Donors rethink aid strategy for rise in militancy," *The Daily Star,* 18 February 2005 at http://www.thedailystar.net/2005/02/18/d5021801022.htm
2. "Donors can leave if they can't adjust to our policy: Saifur grills them for 'political interference'," *The Daily Star,* 17 March 2005 at http://www.thedailystar.net/2005/03/17/d5031701022.htm

3. Anand Kumar, "Bangladesh Mellows Sensing Possible Economic Benefits from the US," *South Asia Analysis Group*, Paper no. 1467, July 22, 2005 at http://www.southasiaanalysis.org/%5Cpapers15%5Cpaper1467.html
4. Saiful Alam, "BNP's dilemma," *The Daily Star*, April 3, 2005 at http://www.thedailystar.net/2005/04/03/d50403020434.htm
5. "Donors warned not to interfere: Says PM in JS, denies Islamist militancy," *The Daily Star*, March 16, 2005 at http://thedailystar.net/2005/03/16/d5031601011.htm
6. Anand Kumar, "Dilemma for Donors in Bangladesh," *South Asia Analysis Group*, Paper no. 1313, March 31, 2005 at http://www.southasiaanalysis.org/%5Cpapers14%5Cpaper1313.html
7. "Govt takes over helm of BDF meet from WB: Apparently to duck donors' pointed queries," *The Daily Star*, 2 March 2005 at http://www.thedailystar.net/2005/03/02/d5030201033.htm
8. "Bangla Bhai not creation of media: Admits Babar," *The Daily Star*, March 7, 2006 at http://www.thedailystar.net/2006/03/07/d6030701033.htm
9. Anand Kumar, "Crackdown On Terror In Bangladesh: Will It Root Out The Menace?," *South Asia Analysis Group*, Paper no. 1725, 8 March 2006 at http://www.southasiaanalysis.org/%5Cpapers18%5Cpaper1725.html
10. US Peace Corps leaves Bangladesh, BBC news, 15 March 2006 at http://news.bbc.co.uk/2/hi/south_asia/4810100.stm
11. Anand Kumar, "Bangladesh : Threat of Terror Continues despite Denials," South Asia Analysis Group, Paper no. 1768, 16 April 2006 at http://www.southasiaanalysis.org/%5Cpapers18%5Cpaper1768.html
12. *Warden Message, Public Announcement*, Embassy of the United States in Dhaka, March 22, 2006 at http://dhaka.usembassy.gov/warden_message_mar22_06.html
13. Anand Kumar, Bangladesh: Attempt to Restrain Islamists before Elections Lacks Sincerity, South Asia Analysis Group, Paper no. 1988, 11 October 2006 at http://www.southasiaanalysis.org/%5Cpapers20%5Cpaper1988.html
14. "Death for Bangladesh 'militants'", *BBC News* 15 August 2006 at http://news.bbc.co.uk/2/hi/south_asia/4794655.stm
15. "3 JMB cadres in Tangail get 12 years RI," *The Daily Star*, September 19, 2006 at http://www.thedailystar.net/2006/09/19/d60919070496.htm
16. "PM sings success of law enforcers: Hopes terrorism to die down with Rahman's arrest," *The Daily Star*, 3 March 2006 at http://www.thedailystar.net/2006/03/03/d6030301022.htm
17. "Roundup: Bangladesh can crush any forms of terrorism: PM," *People's Daily*, March 3, 2006 at http://english.peopledaily.com.cn/200603/03/eng20060303_247459.html
18. "We don't harbour terrorists: Bangladesh," The Indjan Express, May 22, 2006 at http://www.expressindia.com/news/fullstory.php?newsid=64752
19. AL leaders involved: Hannan tells court about Kotalipara plot to kill Hasina, *The Daily Star*, May 14, 2010 at http://www.thedailystar.net/newDesign/news-details.php?nid=138377
20. Julfikar Ali Manik, LeT grenades let terror loose, *The Daily Star*, January 28, 2011 at http://www.thedailystar.net/newDesign/news-details.php?nid=171859
21. HuJI leader admits to 2004 attack targeting Sheikh Hasina, *The Times of India*, Nov 2, 2007, at http://articles.timesofindia.indiatimes.com/2007-11-02/rest-of-world/27993006_1_sheikh-hasina-grenade-attack-huji
22. Voicebox, *The Daily Star*, December 19, 2008 at http://www.thedailystar.net/magazine/2008/12/02/voice.htm

23. "War Crimes Law and the Constitution," Central Publicity Department, Jamaat-e-Islami Bangladesh, Dhaka, February 2008.
24. Since 1991, the Islamists, particularly the Jamaat-e-Islami has maintained close contacts with the two main political parties (Awami Leagu and BNP) and switched sides more than once until they entered into an electoral alliance with the BNP. Please see, Ali Riaz, *Islamist Militancy in Bangladesh: A Complex Web,* Routledge, London, p. 41.
25. Monideepa Banerjee, "Hasina pledges to root out terror," *NDTv*, 31 December, 2008, at http://www.ndtv.com/convergence/ndtv/story.aspx?id=NEWEN20080078352&ch=12/31/2008%2010:17:00%20PM, also see "Advani welcomes Hasina's statement on terror," *The Hindu*, 2 January 2009 at http://www.hindu.com/thehindu/holnus/002200901021605.htm
26. Anand Kumar, "Sheikh Hasina's Regional Anti-Terror Task Force Unlikely to Takeoff," *IDSA Comments,* March 16, 2009 at http://www.idsa.in/idsastrategiccomments/SheikhHasinasRegionalAntiTerrorTaskForceUnlikelytoTakeoff_AKumar_160309
27. 'Armed force will turn B'desh into Gaza', *IBN Live*, February 12, 2009 at http://content.ibnlive.in.com/article/12-Feb-2009world/antiterror-force-not-good-for-bangladesh-opposition-85133-2.html, also see "Anti-terror force will turn Bangladesh into Gaza: Opposition," *Thaindian News*, 12 February 2009 at http://www.thaindian.com/newsportal/politics/anti-terror-force-will-turn-bangladesh-into-gaza-opposition_100154089.html
28. "Anti-terror taskforce will invite trouble, says Nizami," *The Financial Express,* 14 February 2009 at http://www.thefinancialexpress-bd.com/2009/02/14/58833.html
29. Mehnaaz Momen, Bangladesh in 2009: The Peril Within, *Asian Survey,* Vol. 50, No. 1, pp. 157-163.
30. "New DGFI chief named," 3 February 2009, at http://dev.bdnews24.com/details.php?id=124567&cid=2
31. Anisur Rahman, "Major Intelligence Shake Up in Bangladesh," PTI, 17 March 2009 at http://news.outlookindia.com/items.aspx?artid=656051
32. Mehnaaz Momen, *op. cit.*
33. Syed Sajjad Ali, "Dhaka hunts N-E rebels on its soil," *Hindustan Times,* April 07, 2009 at http://www.hindustantimes.com/StoryPage/Print/398064.aspx
34. Praveen Swamy, "Bangladesh foils 26/11 anniversary plot," *The Hindu*, 25 November 2009 at http://www.thehindu.com/news/article54428.ece
35. Haroon Habib, "Another Lashkar suspect held in Dhaka," *The Hindu,* 23 November 2009 at http://www.thehindu.com/news/international/article53226.ece, also see "Latest LeT catch a 'recruiter, arms expert'" 23 November 2009 BDnews24.com at http://bdnews24.com/details.php?id=147560&cid=3
36. Shariful Islam, "2 Lashkar men held inside Indian border: They slipped into Bangladesh to lead 15-member commando squad; plan was to attack US, Indian embassies on Nov 26" *The Daily Star,* 24 November 2009 at http://www.thedailystar.net/newDesign/news-details.php?nid=115334
37. Caesar Mandal, "Terrorists on the run after Bangla crackdown," *The Times of India,* 24 November 2009 at http://articles.timesofindia.indiatimes.com/2009-11-24/kolkata/28060546_1_jmb-rab-officials-rapid-action-battalion
38. Caesar Mandal, "Terrorists on the run after Bangla crackdown," *The Times of India,* 24 November 2009 at http://articles.timesofindia.indiatimes.com/2009-11-24/kolkata/28060546_1_jmb-rab-officials-rapid-action-battalion
39. "Ghulam Azam urged ME not to recognise Bangladesh: Prosecution tells war tribunal," *The Daily Star,* 16 February 2012, http://www.thedailystar.net/newDesign/news-details.php?nid=222589

40. Julfikar Ali Manik and Rizanuzzaman Laskar, "Ghulam Azam indicted: 5 war crime charges framed against him; trial to start June 5," *The Daily Star*, 14 May 2012 at http://www.thedailystar.net/newDesign/news-details.php?nid=234060, also see Haroon Habib, "Jamaat founder indicted for war crimes," The Hindu, 13 May 2012 at http://www.thehindu.com/news/international/article3415722.ece?css=print
41. "Bangladesh Islamic party leaders indicted for alleged atrocities committed during 1971 war," *The Washington Post*, 28 May 2012 at http://www.washingtonpost.com/world/asia_pacific/bangladesh-islamic-party-leaders-indicted-on-war-crimes-charges-for-their-roles-in-1971-war/2012/05/28/gJQAttiwvU_story.html, also see Julfikar Ali Manik and Rizanuzzaman Laskar, "War Crimes Trial: Nizami, Mollah indicted," *The Daily Star*, 29 May 2012 at http://www.thedailystar.net/newDesign/news-details.php?nid=236144
42. "Trail of 7 war crimes suspects may finish by Dec: Shafique," The Daily Star, July 31, 2012 at http://www.thedailystar.net/newDesign/latest_news.php?nid=39570
43. "Raise voice against move to protect war criminals: PM asks sector commanders," *The Daily Star*, 27 February 2012 at http://www.thedailystar.net/newDesign/news-details.php?nid=224054
44. "ULFA Chairman Rajkhowa held in Bangladesh, flown to Delhi," *Hindustan Time*, 3 December 2009 at http://www.hindustantimes.com/News-Feed/India/ULFA-Chairman-Rajkhowa-held-in-Bangladesh-flown-to-Delhi/Article1-482481.aspx
45. Manosh Das and Pankaj Borthakur, "Bangladesh pushes back three top Ulfa leaders," *The Times of India*, 5 February 2011 at http://articles.timesofindia.indiatimes.com/2011-02-05/guwahati/28372775_1_ulfa-leaders-chitraban-hazarika-sasadhar-choudhury#ixzz1DFPDd5X1
46. Anand Kumar, "Crackdown on Northeast Insurgents: Dhaka Prepares for Hasina's India Visit," *IDSA Comments*, November 18, 2009 at http://www.idsa.in/idsacomments/CrackdownonNortheastInsurgents_DhakaPreparesforHasinasIndiaVisit_akumar_181109

8

Towards a New Beginning

The Awami League government, led by Sheikh Hasina, came with a very clear-cut perspective regarding the future of Bangladesh. They knew very well that the anti-liberation forces had gathered strength after the assassination of Sheikh Mujibur Rahman in August 1975. The BNP led four-party alliance government had tried to revive obscurantist, Islamist forces in the country, which had failed Bangladesh in the past and caused lot of suffering to its people. What was worse, they had tried to target the top leadership of Awami League, whom they considered as being secular and friendly towards India. This approach of extremists was very similar to the one they had taken during the liberation war, by murdering all the top intellectuals of Bangladesh.

During the BNP led four party regime Islamists gathered strength because they received active support of Jamaat. The law enforcement agencies of state, police and military were politicised. Even after countrywide bombing instead of cracking down, the police were under direction not to harass certain people, who were actually involved in terror activities. Political parties were using terrorists to settle political scores or to neutralize political adversaries.

Thus the law enforcement agencies were attuned not to take serious actions. Even when they were under tremendous pressure to act, only cosmetic measures were taken. Immediately after a terror attack would take place, the BNP and allies used to politicize the incident. The law enforcement agencies were getting confused. Incidents like Kotalipara where Sheikh Hasina was attacked were not successfully investigated. The BNP used to issue a not to be touched list which often included wanted terrorists and their patrons.

Clearly in these circumstances it was impossible for law enforcement agencies to perform and show result.

Fortunately, the Sheikh Hasina government has changed all this. Not only has state patronage to terrorism been withdrawn, but the law enforcement agencies have been given clear instructions to go after the terrorist groups. This approach was now possible because several Awami League leaders were killed in terror attacks. Even Sheikh Hasina faced several attacks on her life. Now it was very clear to Hasina that if Awami League as a political party has to survive in its present form then it must act against Islamist radical groups. The thumping majority in parliament only further strengthened this resolve. During her previous term, Sheikh Hasina was hamstrung and could not act against terrorist groups because of her dependence on other groups.

Hasina also knows that this is the last opportunity to bring war criminals and murderers of her father to book. This action too is not possible unless her government decides to go after extremists. Thus now state support to extremism is not available. On the other hand, state is working to counter this phenomenon.

The political philosophy of Awami League is now clearer than ever. It has no love lost for the Islamists. The clear instructions given to the law enforcement agencies are helping them to go after extremists in a professional way. And the results can now be seen. The same police force has been able to bust modules of JMB and HuJI in Bangladesh as well as the local modules of international outfits like LeT and Jaish. Some major terror incidents have been averted. Their south Asia wide network has been exposed.

However, this is also not to suggest that only the withdrawal of state support would be able to fully defeat the phenomenon of extremism. The rise of extremism is also an independent process, often supported by international actors. In this the role of ISI, Gulf charities and Western charities becomes important. A large part of expatriate Bangladeshi population is exposed to the Wahabi Islam prevailing in many Gulf countries. The government is also trying to check these forces that have already done lot of damage. Though the state is on a damage control path, it remains to be seen how successful they will be in this effort.

Domestically, Qaumi madrassas have been instrumental in spreading extremism. Though an attempt is being made to improve the situation, but again this would be a daunting task.

Extremist organistions like Jamaat have been able to gain acceptance and spread their reach in Bangladesh by offering various social and economic services to the poor people. As state institutions were decaying corruption had become rampant making it easy for the Jamaat and institutions nurtured by it to occupy the space vacated by the state. They want to further entrench themselves by attacking the functioning institutions of the state like judiciary and even the NGOs.

It will be a very arduous and difficult task for any government in Bangladesh to revive and strengthen state institutions and deliver to the people. Ensuring good governance in all South Asian states has been a challenge. The long term success of the state against Islamic radicalism would depend on how the Bangladesh state manages to strengthen itself.

Lack of Domestic Consensus

The existence of two parallel political philosophies in Bangladesh has created tensions in post liberation Bangladesh. One wants a religiously tolerant Bangladesh if not a fully secular Bangladesh. The other wants an Islamic future for Bangladesh. The struggle between Bengali and Bangladeshi nationalism is chiefly because of this. The scene has been further complicated by the strengthening of Islamist groups who are not satisfied only with Islamic future, but want an Islamic state in the country where governance is done in accordance with Sharia.

Though Islamic parties do not get more than 5 to 7 per cent of the total votes, they have emerged as the kingmakers. Even in December 2008 elections, where the BNP was wiped out and the Jamaat got fewer seats, the percentage of votes polled by Jamaat actually increased.

It is true that there was always a section of the BNP that was opposed to the Islamists and the Jamaat, this section is now getting increasingly marginalised. Whenever this section tried to draw the attention of party bosses to the activities of extremist elements, they had to face their wrath. In the 2001 elections BNP had majority on its own and Jamaat had just 17 MPs, despite which Khaleda Zia gave Jamaat ministers considerable space which they used to promote the Islamisation of the country. It was because of the presence of Islamist parties in the coalition that no action was taken against the terror groups like HuJI and JMB. On the other hand even leaders of BNP tried to use them to settle political scores with Awami League leaders. Involvement of Mufti Hannan in attack on Sheikh Hasina was an example of this. These challenges are no less significant if Bangladesh wants to win its struggle against extremism.

Sheikh Hasina government has acted not only against the radical groups in Bangladesh, it has also taken steps against Indian Insurgent Groups (IIGs).

These groups have been using Bangladeshi territory to launch operations against India. Besides, Bangladesh was also used as a transit route for supplying arms and ammunition to northeast insurgent groups.

Taking action against IIGs was not easy as for long Bangladesh had denied existence of such groups. Any action against them would have contradicted this. But to the credit of Sheikh Hasina government, it must be said, that they managed to overcome this and took decisive action against such groups. Their sincerity was shown when they handed over many insurgent leaders even in the absence of any extradition treaty.

During her last tenure Sheikh Hasina was not able to act with full success against IIGs because she did not have full control over law enforcement agencies and the military. This time however, things are different. This Hasina government came to power after the two year rule of the caretaker government. This caretaker government was backed by Gen Moeen who made some remarkable changes in the Bangladesh army. He publically stated that the army in Bangladesh was subservient to the democratic government.

This was new in Bangladeshi politics whereby army was voluntarily giving up its political interference. This also gave Hasina an opportunity to exercise considerable control over the army which had been absent during earlier democratic regimes. Her action against IIGs and Islamists were far more successful because she got lot of support from army and other law enforcement agencies.

Hesitant Approach to Bring Back Secularism

The battle to strengthen moderate Islam in Bangladesh needs to be fought at many levels. If law enforcement agencies need a free hand to act against the terrorist outfits, then they also need a proper legal and legislative framework in which to operate. This has been realised by the Awami League government.

Attempt was made to bury secularism which was one of the four pillars on which the independent Bangladesh was founded. The military regimes had tried to do this by the passing of the Fifth Amendment by Zia-ur-Rahman and the Eighth Amendment by General Ershad which declared Islam as the state religion. These measures legitimised Jamaat whose top leaders were seen as war criminals.

The Supreme Court of Bangladesh has now struck down both these amendments. During the electioneering Awami League had promised that it would act against the war criminals. It also promised to stop misuse of religion in politics. The party has now an opportunity to fulfill this promise.

The apex court of Bangladesh has also upheld the 29 August 2005 judgment of a three-judge bench led by Justice ABM Khairul Haque which declared the Fifth Amendment to the country's constitution as "void ab initio and illegal".[1] This is a significant development in a country where Islamists have been threatening to establish their sway.

At the same time, however, it is also important to note that the government has decided to keep the words "Bismillah-Ar-Rahman-Ar-Rahim" in the preamble to the constitution and the declaration of Islam as state religion. Sheikh Hasina stated that these things have been retained as they reflect the beliefs of the people. She advised her alliance leaders to accept the reality that the majority of the population in Bangladesh was Muslim. Though secularism has not been fully restored in Bangladesh Sheikh Hasina is of the view that the spirit of the constitution would be restored with the High Courts verdict.[2]

This cautious return to secularism in Bangladesh reflects the political realism of the Awami League. The party knows that in the last several decades Islamist tendencies have taken root among a section of the people and these will not go away overnight. The arch rivals of Awami League always say that Islam would be in danger if Awami League comes to power. Though there is no threat to Islam per-se in Bangladesh as 90 percent of its population is Muslim, still Awami League knows that turning the clock back is not going to be easy. Hence it has made cautious move to restore secularism while leaving Islam as state religion of Bangladesh.

The failure to successfully prosecute war criminals was one important factor that led to revival of extremism in the country. This probably created a feeling among the extremists that their anti-national action would be tolerated even during the present times. This also prompted them to intensify terrorist activities within Bangladesh. The Sheikh Hasina government however now appears determined to remove this anomaly. She has started the process of war crime trial knowing fully well that this could also mean trouble for her government. Islamists in alliance with the BNP have tremendous muscle power and ability to create chaos in the country.

The government of Sheikh Hasina needs to be appreciated for the risk it is taking by prosecuting war criminals. Already reports have appeared in international media that the prosecution of war criminals could bring chaos to Bangladesh. But the Awami League government is going ahead with the trials. The government however is alive to the danger that is posed by this. Hence they have also sought international help in trying war criminals.

Terror Down But Not Out

The actions taken by Sheikh Hasina have weakened extremist and terrorist forces. But they have not been evicted from the country. In many cases, they have gone underground. Their funding is intact. Their networks are is also largely intact. There is no doubt, that in checking Islamic radicalism in Bangladesh, the resolve of Sheikh Hasina and the overwhelming majority she achieved during elections has played a major role. But if this phenomenon is to be defeated the resolve should percolate down to second rung of Awami League leaders also. This fight should not remain Sheikh Hasina's fight only.

There have been a number of developments in Bangladesh which created an environment for action against religious extremist groups and Indian insurgent groups. Its impact is palpable and could be seen on ground. It has led to surrender of insurgents and busting of many trans-national terrorist modules acting from Bangladesh. Modules have been busted even in India on the basis of information gathered from them. It has averted many terror attacks in Bangladesh. This is a remarkable development in south Asia which has a blood-stained history of trans-border terrorism and religious extremism.

The present approach of Bangladesh however is largely focused on 'law and order/force' based. This approach can only be a short-term approach to containing terror. But to completely get rid of this menace Bangladesh will have to widen its counter-terrorism strategy. The country will also have to pay attention to social, political and constitutional, religious and cultural as well as economic and developmental aspects.

Religious extremism is not limited to any one country. Often extremist groups in one country have regional and global links with other outfits. Hence it is necessary to have the support of other countries to comprehensively deal with terrorism. The cooperation between India and Bangladesh indicated that similar support from other countries would yield better results. In South Asia, so far cooperation at a regional level has not been very successful. Certain countries deem terrorist outfits to be 'strategic assets'. This misplaced notion has not allowed them to work in tandem with other countries and this is likely hamper the efforts of countries like Bangladesh and India.

The cooperation between Bangladesh and India to fight terror is noteworthy. This has also produced significant results and dealt a major blow to Islamist groups as well as Northeast insurgents. Though this cooperation is admirable, it has still not reached a level seen in the case of India and Bhutan, where security forces of both countries launched coordinated assault against the terrorists in their respective territories leaving little room for terrorists to escape. However, the cooperation with Bangladesh should not be underestimated.

The only question that remains is whether the present approach of Bangladesh towards terror groups would last and be followed by all political parties across the political spectrum. Bangladeshi politicians have to decide whether they want to identify with the liberation forces or the anti-liberation forces. The direction taken by the country would depend upon the choices its political leaders make. After the October 2008 elections, there was introspection within the BNP, on whether to ally with the radical groups or not, especially when they were still trying to come to terms with enormity of their defeat. But that seems to be history now. The BNP has now resolved its dilemma and has once again tied up with Jamaat. This orientation of BNP can only be reversed if the people give sustained verdict against such policies and anti liberation forces.

NOTES

1. Please see text of Supreme Court verdict on two petitions challenging a 2005 High Court ruling that declared the constitution's Fifth Amendment illegal at http://www.bdnews24.com/image/5th%20Amendment.pdf also see "SC dismisses Fifth Amendment petitions ", *bdnews24.com,* 2 February 2010 at http://www.bdnews24.com/details.php?cid=2&id=152654&hb=1 also see, Haroon Habib, Restoring Bangladesh's core values, *The Hindu,* 2 August 2010 at http://www.thehindu.com/opinion/lead/article546258.ece?homepage=true
2. Anand Kumar, "The Cautious Handling of Secularism in Bangladesh," *IDSA Comments,* 19 January 2010 at http://www.idsa.in/idsacomments/TheCautiousHandlingofSecularisminBangladesh_akumar_190110

Appendix I

Islamic Parties Contesting Polls—Based on Record of Bangladesh Election Commission

1. Jamaat-e-Islami Bangladesh
2. Bangladesh Islami Front
3. Bangladesh Khelafat Andolon
4. Bangladesh Krishak Raj Islami Party
5. Bangladesh Muslim League (Jamir Ali)
6. Bangladesh Tanjimul Islam
7. Islami Al Zihad Dal
8. Islami Oikya Jote which is an alliance of seven parties
9. Islami Shashantantro Andolon
10. Islamic Dal
11. Zaker Party
12. Jamiate Ulumaye Islami Bangladesh
13. People's Muslim Party
14. Quran Sunna Bastabayan Party
15. Quran Darshan Sangstha Bangladesh
16. Tehrikya Ulama-e-Bangladesh
17. Islami Dal Bangladesh (Saifur)
18. Bangladesh Inquilab Party
19. Bangladesh Islami Republican Party
20. Muslim People Party
21. Bangladesh Khelafat Party
22. Muslim League (Yousuf)
23. Muslim League (Matin)
24. Muslim League (Quader)
25. Jamayate Ulamaye Islami Front

Islamic parties and organisations in Existence Between 1964 and 1970—Based on Records of Bangladesh Intelligence

1. Nezam-e-Islam
2. Jamaat-e-Islami
3. Muslim Affairs
4. Jamiyat-e-Ulama-e-Islam

5. Jamiat-e-Ahle Hadith
6. Islami Darodi Sangha
7. United Islamic Front
8. Islami Sangram Parishad
9. Islami Durmuz Party
10. Jatiya Mujaheed Sangha
11. Jamayat-e-Tabligue-e-Deen

Islamic Parties and Organisations Floated Since 1976—Based on Records of Bangladesh Intelligence Agencies

1. Islamic Democratic League
2. Young Muslim Society
3. Islami Oikya Andolan
4. Bangladesh Islami Mohila Mojlish
5. Muslim Shanti Parishad
6. Zikir Ul Dal Bangladesh
7. Bangladesh Muslim League
8. Islami Awami Party
9. Sorbadaliya Islami Sangram Parishad
10. Mojaheed Bahini
11. Bangladesh Muslim Jubo Sangha
12. Bangladesh Jatiya Olama Dal
13. Ittehadul Ullah
14. Islamic Revolution Council
15. Islami Sanghati Parishad
16. Nikhil Bangladesh Muslim League
17. Jamaat-e-Islami Bangladesh (Jabbar)
18. Islami Jatiya Oikya Jote
19. Islamic Republican Party
20. Al Qudds of Bangladesh
21. Islami Jubo Shibir
22. Bangladesh Olama Front
23. Muslim Akida Association
24. Idara-e-Hefazat-e-Islam
25. Islami Jukto Front
26. Bangladesh Islami Parishad
27. Hizbul Qurrah Bangladesh
28. Progatishil Islami
29. Muslim Millat Shariat
30. Islami Hukumat Bastabayan
31. Islami Shashantantra Andolan

32. Rabiat Al Alam Alah Alam
33. 27-party Islami Sanghati Jote
34. Islami Dawati Sangstha
35. Anjuman-e-Tahfuz-e-Arkan-e-Islam, Ahle Sunnatul Jamaat,
36. Muslim Oikya League
37. Muhajer Qawmi Movement
38. Bangladesh Khelafat Majlish
39. Jamiyate Hijbullah
40. Bangladesh Mujahedeen
41. Bangladesh Majlish-e-Islam, Bangladesh Islami Biplobi Andolan
42. Jatiya Olama Party
43. Bishaw Muslim Jubo Andolan
44. Islami Oikya Jote
45. Bishaw Muslim Biplobi Council
46. Olama Ekram Party
47. Khelafat Party
48. Tahfuz-e-Harmain
49. Bangladesh Khelafat Jubo Andolan
50. Islami Solidarity Party
51. Bangladesh Sunni Front
52. World Mulsim United Forum
53. Bangladesh Sufi Majlish
54. Olama Committee
55. Bangladesh Muslim Oikya Front
56. Islam O Rashtrodrohi Protirodh Morcha
57. Islami Sangram Parishad
58. Bangladesh Muslim Ganotantrik Dal
59. Harkatul Ansar group
60. Al Markajul Islam
61. Bangladesh Hijbut Tahrir
62. Iman Akida Sangrokkhan Committee
63. Hujbul Mahdi
64. Shahadat-e-Al Hiqma
65. Majlish-e-Dawat-ul-Haq
66. Khelafat-e-Rabbani Party
67. Khademul Islam Jamaat
68. Majlish-e-Tahaffuj-e-Khatm-e-Nabuat
69. Faraezi Jamaat

Source: Shakhawat Liton, Islamic parties boom after 1976 ban lifting: Record shows about 100 organisations exist, The Daily Star, 29 August, 2006 at http://www.thedailystar.net/2006/08/29/d6082901022.htm

APPENDIX II

According to the Awami League website following 33 militant terrorist groups are active in Bangladesh:

1. Jama'atul Mujaheedin Bangladesh
2. Shahdat-E-Al Hikma
3. Jamat-E-Yeaheya-Al-Turat
4. Hizbut Touhid
5. Al-Harat-Al–Islamia
6. Al-Markajul-Al-Islami
7. Jamatul Faliaya
8. Touhidi Janata
9. International Islami Front
10. Jummatul-Al-Sadat
11. Shahadat-E-Naboyed
12. Harkatul Zihad
13. Allahar Dal
14. Joisea Mustafa Bangladesh
15. Al-Zihad Bangladesh
16. World Islamic front for Zihad
17. Joisea Mohammed
18. Jamat-ul-Muzahidul Bangladesh
19. Warot Islamic front
20. Jamat-us-Sadat
21. Al-Khidmat
22. Jagrato Muslim Janata Bangladesh (JMJB)
23. Harkot-E-Islam-Al-Zihad
24. Hizbullah Islami Shomaj
25. Muslim Millat Sharia Council
26. Ahele Hadith
27. Hizbul Mahadi
28. Basbid

29. Hizbut Tahrir
30. Al-Quaida
31. Al-Islam Martyrs Brigade
32. International Khotme Noboyet Movement
33. Amora Dhakabashi

Besides the above 33 militant fanatic terrorist groups, the Rohingya refugees coming from Arakan Province of Myanmar also indulged in terrorist activities in the Cox's Bazaar area in different names.

Source: "Sudden Government Partial Crack-down on two of the Islamic Militants and the mystery behind it," Newsletter, Vol. 4. No. 4, April 13, 2005, Bangladesh Awami League Publication at http://www.albd.org/newsletter/2005/vol4_no4_2005.htm

Index